"The lojong teachings on working with destabilizing emotions are Tibet's great gift to a world in desperate need of them. In *Stop Biting the Tail You're Chasing* we hear the wise and patient voice of Anyen Rinpoche, fully immersed in these teachings as only a Tibetan tulku can be, along with his longtime collaborator, Allison Choying Zangmo, kindly speaking to us about how to apply this wisdom to our contemporary lives. Though the teachings are subtle and profound, this is a simple, accessible, and inspiring discussion. This is a book I will read again and again."

—NORMAN FISCHER, poet, Zen priest,
and co-author of *What Is Zen?*

"There is no better way to bring intelligence, sanity, and love into the world than moving away from fixating on the self, and instead, working for the well-being of others. In *Stop Biting the Tail You're Chasing*, Anyen Rinpoche and Allison Choying Zangmo present us with a fresh, insightful, and engaging look at the most essential, practical, and potent instructions on how to do just that—the lojong or mind training teachings. I think you will find this book a great guide on how to move through the world with joy and grace."

—ELIZABETH MATTIS NAMGYAL,
author of *The Power of an Open Question*

Stop Biting the Tail You're Chasing

Stop Biting the Tail You're Chasing

Using Buddhist Mind Training to Free Yourself from Painful Emotional Patterns

ANYEN RINPOCHE AND
ALLISON CHOYING ZANGMO

SHAMBHALA
Boulder • 2018

Shambhala Publications, Inc.
4720 Walnut Street
Boulder, Colorado 80301
www.shambhala.com

The *Heart Sutra* on pages 141–44 is from *The Heart Sutra: An Oral Teaching* by Geshe Sonam Rinchen, translated and edited by Ruth Sonam (Boston: Snow Lion, 2003). Used by permission.

9 8 7 6 5 4 3 2 1

FIRST EDITION

Printed in the United States of America

♾ This edition is printed on acid-free paper that meets the American National Standards Institute z39.48 Standard.

♻ This book is printed on 30% postconsumer recycled paper. For more information please visit www.shambhala.com.

Distributed in the United States by Penguin Random House LLC and in Canada by Random House of Canada Ltd

Designed by Steve Dyer

LIBRARY OF CONGRESS CATALOGING-IN-PUBLICATION DATA
Names: Anyen, Rinpoche, author.
Title: Stop biting the tail you're chasing: using Buddhist mind training to free yourself from painful emotional patterns / Anyen Rinpoche and Allison Choying Zangmo.
Description: First Edition. | Boulder: Shambhala, 2018.
Identifiers: LCCN 2017049077 | ISBN 9781611805710 (pbk.: alk. paper)
Subjects: LCSH: Blo-sbyong. | Emotions—Religious aspects—Buddhism.
Classification: LCC BQ7805.A59 2018 | DDC 294.3/444—dc23
LC record available at https://lccn.loc.gov/2017049077

Lord of Sages, Great Lifeforce of the doctrine
of transmission and realization.
Seer of the ultimate essence, Treasury of the
dharma of the Kama and Terma.
Holder of the saffron robes, and our supremely
renowned, resplendent protector.
I pray to Thubten Chokyi Drakpa.

— Composed by Alek Zenkar Rinpoche

Contents

Introduction

I F W E H A V E S P E N T any time reading Buddhist texts, we may be tempted to approach Buddhism from a primarily intellectual standpoint. We may use it as a kind of philosophy that can help us make sense of our incredibly painful lives or as a fresh perspective on reality. But the amazing thing about the dharma is that it is inherently practical, deeply personal, and wholly applicable in the modern world. No matter what difficulties we face in our lives, the dharma can not only help us cope with them, but it can also help us find the richness in those difficult circumstances. It can help us awaken to further possibilities and experience life as a wish-fulfilling gem.

Engaging in the practice of Buddhism demands that we work very directly with our emotions. It requires broad and exacting self-examination and the willingness to chip away at the habits we have formed that perpetuate suffering in ourselves and others. The Buddhist tradition calls this practical, transformative style of practice *lojong*, or mind training. Mind training is an extremely effective style of practice passed down from many of the great Kadampa and bodhisattva masters of old, such as Jowo Je Atisha and Shantideva. As we'll learn in the chapters that follow, these masters took very deliberate, specific actions to train themselves not to engage in painful emotional habits, to increase their compassion for others, and to let go of their own self-cherishing.

As the dharma has been passed from Tibet to the West over the past several decades, lojong has been introduced by different spiritual masters, often as a set of slogans that can be used to kindle mindfulness. While these slogans are part of the tradition of lojong, mind training is actually a vast topic. In fact, which of the teachings in the entirety of Buddhism could be excluded from lojong? All of Buddhism is mind training, as Buddhism has no goal other than personal transformation, growth, and ultimately liberation and the cessation of suffering for ourselves and others.

This book is meant to provide a set of tools that you can apply in daily life to gradually relieve your own suffering and extend that relief to others. It is our greatest hope that you pick up these tools, experiment with them, and continually use the ones that work. With gentle and consistent effort, we are all capable of experiencing the joy and happiness that result from liberating ourselves from the torrent of emotional conflict. That freedom, in turn, can naturally be shared and enjoyed by the beings we encounter each and every day.

Stop Biting the Tail You're Chasing

1

The Emotions as
Friends and Enemies

A RE THE EMOTIONS our best friends or our worst enemies? Most of the time, we are not sure. In Western culture, we are generally taught, either directly or by example, to
dive into the emotions or go to battle with them. We see people
in the world around us relating to their emotions in one of these
two extreme approaches—sometimes even both at once. Many
of us choose one approach or the other, or wind up somewhere
in between.

Three Ordinary Approaches to
Dealing with the Emotions

What does it mean to treat the emotions as friends? Simply put, it
means that we relate to our emotions more easily—or maybe just
more—than we relate to the people in our lives. It means that we
engage in an emotional dialogue with ourselves about the range
of what we feel and why we feel that way. We may feel others
don't understand us, and we wish to understand ourselves better
to fill the void of intimacy in our lives.

Focusing on the emotions may serve several purposes. We
may think that if we can just understand our emotions better,

we'll naturally be able to handle their intensity more effectively. We may think we'll stop being hurt by the emotions that arise from certain situations or behaviors that seem to surface again and again in our lives. In other words, for us highly emotional beings, the intellectual mind may be able to intervene in areas that have previously been dominated by the emotions in order to free us from their grip. We also may have the idea that understanding our emotions will enable us to resolve old emotions and resentments by revisiting past wounds with more strength and wisdom than we had before. We may feel this will help us change in the future, or help us let go of events in our lives that have dominated much of our mental and emotional energy.

Many of us may feel extremely positive about relating to the emotions as friends, even though we are probably aware on some level that much of our emotional energy is wrapped up in feeling dissatisfied and unhappy. Reflect on the words of one American woman who said, "I used to think that I didn't want to feel unhappiness. But then I realized that if I didn't feel deep unhappiness, I wouldn't be capable of deep happiness. I realized that I want to be a whole person who feels a full range of emotions. That's what makes life meaningful." Her words give voice to something that many of us believe: without the emotions, we wouldn't be who we are. We wouldn't know why life is worth living or what is worth living for.

But this is only one way that we relate to the emotions. Many of us don't spend a lot of time and energy trying to decipher how we feel. Instead, we treat the emotions as enemies. This approach also expresses itself in a variety of ways. For some, emotions are just a waste of time. They may get in the way of ambitions or responsibilities we have in life. If we are scientifically minded, we may feel that spending time relating to our feelings is of no benefit. Others of us may have been overwhelmed by specific emotional reactions toward things that happened in the past. We have learned to shut ourselves down. We may avoid getting close to others, and we may push down whatever feelings start to come up inside of us. Because we mentally and emotionally disassociate from what is going on inside of us, we may also become foggy about the thoughts and feelings of others. When we feel disconnected, we may unknowingly perpetuate that feeling and stay disconnected. We may avoid our feelings by doing something too much—eating, drinking, sex, drugs, television. We may ignore, withdraw, or isolate.

Finally, some of us move between the two extremes. Our lives are characterized by periods when we feel emotionally awake and alive, although perhaps too intensely so. During those times, we may remain connected to our feelings and even attempt to dialogue with ourselves about what is happening with our emotions. But at a certain point, the energy of the emotions may become too much to handle. We begin to distance ourselves from our emotions and others, trying to remain suspended in time and space, to find safety, or to protect ourselves from what we think and feel. Or maybe we are simply exhausted from trying to keep our energy balanced. Our imbalances manifest in all sorts of ways. Some of us move between anxiety and depression. Some of us can't relax and don't sleep. Some of us just sink into a deep emotional abyss.

We may wonder if our emotions are as dangerous as we think they are. They can certainly feel dangerous, and their expression can feel foreboding. Our emotions are part of an incredibly powerful energy pattern that moves throughout the entire body. The movement of the emotions affects both the body and mind. Some of us might experience emotional patterns with energy so intense that it seems to last, without moving, for months at a time. We may want to protect ourselves from falling into a state of mind that we are not sure we can get out of. Treating the emotions as enemies, or ignoring them, isn't necessarily a bad solution in the face of this kind of danger.

The Buddhist Approach:
Beyond Friends and Enemies

Of these three approaches, which is the healthiest? From the perspective of the Buddhist teachings, we may frame the question slightly differently. Instead of wondering which approach is healthiest, we could instead ask which brings the most happiness. After all, none of the approaches described above likely brings us much joy or happiness in itself. In each of the three approaches described above, we are merely managing our energy to achieve a certain result. In the first scenario, we allow ourselves to embrace our emotions, even inducing the "highs" of life, and *accept* that this means we'll also experience deep "lows." We know from our own experience that life is mostly filled with lows. The moments when we truly feel we are getting what we want are few and far between and interspersed with unhappy or dissatisfactory situations. So in order to remain close to our emotions, we fully embrace the depth of our emotional sensitivity, which can be extremely painful. As we'll discuss in later chapters, it takes great skill for spiritual practitioners to find balance with their own emotional sensitivity.

In the second scenario, we shut down the depths of our feelings, both our positive emotions, such as love, joy, and happiness, and our painful emotions, such as sadness and disappointment. We may feel numb, disconnected, or lonely, or we may simply pass the time being occupied by the tasks of ordinary life.

In the third scenario, we are walking a tightrope, moving between one extreme and another, trying not to have an accident. But managing emotional highs and lows is always difficult and unpredictable, and our actions and interactions with others are often precipitous in the process.

From where does happiness stem? We can consider the answer to this question in the most general manner. The Buddhist teachings say that all human beings wish to be happy and that our common definition of happiness is getting the things that we want and avoiding the things that we don't want. We can probably relate to this way of thinking; it is a thought pattern that we have in common with every single being on this planet. But if we contemplate this subject deeply, we find that this kind of worldly happiness can never be achieved. We simply aren't able to engineer our lives to the degree that nothing unwanted or painful ever happens to us. Yet this fact is difficult for us to accept. Whether we realize it or not, most of our time and energy is used to avoid this reality. We persist in thinking the same way that we always have: *If I can just do it this way . . . If he or she will act like this . . . If it works out just perfectly this time . . .* We base our hopes of future happiness on the belief that things will ultimately come together in just the right way, or that the things that didn't work out well this time can be made better in the future, or that we'll finally enjoy the positive results of our hard work. But how many times has this actually happened? And when it did, how many times were we truly happy about the result, and how long did that happiness actually last? Probably not long.

The Buddhist view of happiness might best be described as contentment. The word *contentment* describes a state of mind in which we are satisfied with what we have — in which we have dropped our ordinary wishes for this or that and are just focused on what we have to work with in this particular moment. When we are content, we aren't passive or disengaged with life. We simply appreciate whatever is happening, maintaining acceptance toward all the various situations that life brings. We feel joy, appreciation, gratitude, and connection with ourselves and others. When emotions arise, they help us know ourselves better and see the areas of our personality and character that still need to develop and mature. The emotions are thus a source of information, an inspiration for spiritual growth, and a measure of our own personal development.

When we are able to relate to the emotions in this balanced way, we can develop genuine contentment. In contrast to what most of us may think, contentment is not a lack of ambition. Rather, it is a healthy kind of ambition that focuses our energy on making the best possible use of every single moment to bring well-being to ourselves and others. When we have the genuine wish to find contentment and to help others do the same, we embody the great altruistic mind of a bodhisattva. Bodhisattvas are spiritual heroes who have the courage to put their own personal wishes and ideas of happiness aside, because they realize that true happiness is achieved by working for the good of others.

The Difficulty of Finding Happiness

We have been mistaken about the definition of happiness all along. The Buddhist teachings tell us that happiness is something that we human beings do not know how to achieve. In his famous text *Way of a Bodhisattva*, the renowned Buddhist master Shantideva (685–763) describes how an ordinary being develops the qualities of a bodhisattva, pointing out that human beings invite the causes of unhappiness to themselves and treat the causes of happiness as their enemies. These words may be surprising because, after all, most of us feel that we are suffering so intensely and we want to be happy more than anything. How could we actually be pushing the happiness we want so much even further away?

First, we should examine the cause of happiness and contentment, according to Shantideva and other great Buddhist masters. According to Shantideva, a quintessential bodhisattva, happiness comes from focusing on ourselves less rather than more. In Buddhism, the conduct of a bodhisattva is concentrated on gradually turning the focus *away* from oneself and *toward* others. By doing this, a bodhisattva is said to bring benefit both to oneself and to others. How does this work?

First, when we directly work in others' interests, we benefit them by helping to place them in a state of happiness and well-being. Second, even when our energy is focused on helping others, our efforts still indirectly benefit us. We may wonder why helping others benefits us. After all, don't we feel better when we focus on ourselves and make sure that our needs are being met? One answer to this question is that we often feel a sense of relaxation, joy, or comfort when we help someone else. Simply put, it feels good to help others. So whenever we help bring relaxation, peace, or happiness to others, we share in their positive state of mind and whatever positive situations they enjoy that we have helped bring about.

We may also resonate with the idea that our positive actions will ripen sooner or later as positive conditions in our own lives. This isn't to suggest that the motivation we have when we look outward and focus on helping others should be selfish—for example, that we should focus on others because then they will repay us by helping us when we need it. To approach helping others with an agenda, or with the wish to be treated in a certain way ourselves now or in the future in reward for that help, would likely only lead to frustration and disappointment. Rather than thinking of the ripening of positive actions as payback, we could instead have a more organic attitude toward the whole process. It makes sense, and it is logical, that when we have positive motivation and engage in positive actions, the results of that motivation and those actions will also be positive now and in the future. In Buddhism, the idea that results ripen similar to their causes is called *karma*, or the law of cause and effect. The law of cause and effect is extremely logical. It says that sooner or later we reap the fruit of whatever kind of seed we sow. The great Buddhist master Jigme Lingpa (1729–1798), one of the sources of the Nyingma lineage of Tibetan Buddhism called the Longchen Nyingthig (Heart Essence of the Vast Expanse) explains it this way:

If the seed is medicinal, the sprout will be medicine.
If the seed is poisonous, the sprout will be poison.

Even though this is true, karma isn't caught up in how things happen to appear at any given moment. It may sometimes seem as if people who do bad things achieve good results in the short term, but according to the law of karma, sooner or later we reap what we sow. This isn't particularly a matter of external reward and punishment by the universe but rather what state of mind we are feeding on the inside. If we make choices in our lives based on greed, jealousy, anger, and so forth, we cultivate that state of mind, and it only grows to torture us further. Likewise, if we train ourselves in positive motivation and actions, the results have a direct impact on our state of being.

Another reason helping others benefits us is because we spend most of our lives looking at ourselves as though through a microscope—thinking, *Is this okay with me? How do I feel right now? Do I have enough? Is what I'm doing good enough? Is he or she treating me well enough?* and so on. This strong habit of always focusing on ourselves is very painful. The result of focusing so hard on ourselves is that we never take breaks from our ambition to achieve the lives that we want, that we think we deserve. We can't find a moment to relax. But when we focus on others, we relax our normal tendency to place ourselves and what we want in the center of everything.

Although we may not realize it, placing ourselves in the center of everything is the greatest cause of all our personal suffering. The more we focus on ourselves, the more we notice what is wrong with what we have, what is difficult about our own lives, and our pervasive dissatisfaction. Making our emotional lives, our feelings and sensitivities, gradually less important brings a great sense of relief. It is like coming up for a breath of air after being underwater for a long time. We all are gasping for air under the pressure of the strong emotions bearing down on us.

We are constricted by our own selfishness and self-centeredness. In the Buddhist teachings, the relief that we feel when we focus on ourselves less is called *decreasing self-attachment*. We define *self-attachment* as grasping at the self, the ego, and our personal identity. Self-attachment can take many forms. It can be expressed as the attachment we have to our own emotions; the attachment we have to how others perceive and treat us; the attachment we have to getting our own way and having the things that we want; or the attachment we have to ourselves as people who deserve kindness, respect, love, and so forth.

Probably the strongest self-attachment we have is our attachment to the physical body and to the emotions. The body, heart, and mind have an intense interconnection, such that feelings felt in the body begin to express mentally and emotionally, and feelings felt in the heart and mind begin to express physically. For example, when we are mentally exhausted, we often become physically ill. Or if we are stressed, we often become emotionally reactive and easily triggered. Even being extremely elated will eventually bring unhealthy consequences. When we ride on a wave of extremely high energy, we will certainly become exhausted and crash sooner or later. No matter what we are feeling at a given moment, if we allow it to overtake us, we will find that being wrapped up in that state of mind will bring an unhealthy or imbalanced result.

The Result of Having Friends and Enemies

What happens when we treat our emotions as friends or enemies? The short answer is that we reinforce a pattern that is sure to end in suffering, because any time we react to a feeling, whether positively or negatively, we make our self-attachment stronger. Treating our emotions as either friends or enemies will never help us to be content and accept the lives that we have. The stronger our self-attachment, the more we suffer. Logically speaking, then, the cause of happiness is found in decreasing our self-attachment. As Shantideva says, we invite the causes of suffering and treat the cause of happiness as our enemy because we make our egos and personal identities stronger day by day, simply by following our ordinary emotional tendency to treat the emotions as friends or enemies. The only way to get out of this vicious cycle is to do something radical, something completely different than we have ever known before. The problem most of us have is that we have no idea what else to do. After all, we are competent, intelligent people. If we knew, wouldn't we have done it already?

Potential solutions abound in the modern world. We can try medication, supplements, diets, teas, and exercise. There are also all kinds of new spiritual teachings, 12-step programs, and programs that focus on mindfulness, all of which may help. We may even have our own personal ideas about how we should change and what that change should look like. But one of the benefits of working with a tradition such as Buddhism is that everything it teaches is tried, true, and timeless. In other words, the Buddhist teachings transcend time and culture, and they apply to anyone who sincerely wants to put them into practice. We can have confidence in the Buddhist path because its teachings and techniques were relied upon by the great spiritual masters of the tradition, in the past as well as now. Following a tradition can help us achieve a sense of trust and relaxation when we try something new, and make us more willing to follow through with it.

As we encounter these timeless Buddhist teachings, we may have questions about what it means to be a realized master of this tradition. Aren't great spiritual masters practicing something more than just focusing on others' happiness? Isn't their realization and wisdom much deeper? Aren't the minds of great spiritual masters different than those of ordinary beings? The answer to these questions is yes and no. Yes, great spiritual masters have achieved wisdom that enables them to transcend ordinary habits and concerns, to approach situations differently than others, and to find inspiring solutions to the mire of ordinary problems. But it is also said that "Buddhas are born from bodhisattvas." There cannot be, and has never been, a Buddha who did not work intensively at training the mind in the ideas and motivation that guide a bodhisattva. It is that training that takes the Buddha from having an ordinary mind to experiencing the great state of wisdom called Buddhahood. To reflect on this can inspire us. We see that the journey to spiritual mastery can start here and now, by taking up the practice of mind training.

The Life of Patrul Rinpoche

The great Buddhist master Patrul Rinpoche (1808–1887) was known to be a highly realized master. There are many magical stories of his realization, such as his having direct understanding of the minds and thoughts of others, and his resting directly in vivid wisdom awareness based on his connection with and devotion to other great masters of the Dzogchen tradition of the Secret Mantrayana, a special and secret style of practice found within the more general Nyingma tradition. Patrul Rinpoche is also the author of one of the most important texts in the Nyingma tradition of Tibetan Buddhism, *Words of My Perfect Teacher*. This text is one of the sources of the Longchen Nyingthig lineage. Like the *Way of a Bodhisattva*, this text is a fundamental source of how to live and practice authentically, in a way that invites a mind full of wisdom and compassion.

Patrul Rinpoche lived in a radical way. He focused solely on the dharma and the good of others. He put no energy or attention into his appearance or personal circumstances. He had no wish to receive attention or respect from others. He wandered here and there, taking no formal title, and he avoided having a permanent home or building a grand place to teach and practice in. He used his beggar's appearance to show people the genuine nature of the dharma, and to express his one-pointed and genuine wish to help others practice the dharma authentically.

A major part of Patrul Rinpoche's life, practice, and study was devoted to the *Way of a Bodhisattva*. He formally received teachings on the text countless times, and he gave teachings on the same throughout his entire lifetime. It is said that after teaching on the *Way of a Bodhisattva* for several consecutive years in the sacred place called Dzogchen Shri Singha in Tibet, vast numbers of the flowers called serchen, flowers with thirty to fifty petals each, bloomed as a sign of the blessings of his profound teaching and practice. These became known as *Way of a Bodhisattva* flowers. This story is a reminder that putting others first is the true source of magic, joy, and contentment. Keeping Patrul Rinpoche's example in mind, we can feel confident that training in bodhisattva conduct will also help us transcend some of the pain and suffering of ordinary life and, if we practice sincerely, raise us to the level of an authentic bodhisattva.

The Approach of Blame

When we reflect honestly, we see that our ordinary mechanism for dealing with difficult, painful, and unwanted situations is quite different from the bodhisattva's approach. While bodhisattvas are focused on others, in an effort to skillfully bring relief to those around them, we tend to place blame on others or things outside of ourselves. This allows us to keep our self-attachment strong, and it keeps us from tearing down the ego even a little bit. This blaming tendency seems to be universal, part of the human instinct to protect ourselves. We simply focus on how things outside of us are unsatisfactory, how they didn't go as planned. Each of us likely has our own unique thought pattern when we are placing blame: *I feel this way because . . . he did this . . . she did that . . . this happened . . . that happened . . .* and so the story goes. Our habit of placing blame is so strong that we do it equally for insignificant situations as well as important ones. For example, we may blame an event or person in the past for a wound that we haven't been able to heal, which causes us to act self-destructively or to feel a lot of physical or emotional pain in a cyclic or obsessive pattern. Equally so, we may blame a reckless or aggressive driver on the road or an unkind word from a friend or colleague for disturbing our state of mind.

But according to the dharma, we are responsible for making ourselves unhappy by attributing so much meaning to our emotions, which are fleeting and unreal, just like a water mirage. We are so attached to the idea of happiness that we blame anyone or anything that appears to interrupt it, not realizing that our own self-attachment is the cause. From the very beginning, we have made a grave mistake about the nature of life. We have thought, emotionally even if not intellectually, that life is supposed to be the way we want it to be. We all have had such grand dreams since we were children. Our parents and teachers taught us that if we work hard, we will be able to achieve our hearts' desires. But ordinary, worldly life doesn't really have a promise of success, fairness, or justice. Sometimes we do everything right. We bend over backward, bringing all the right circumstances together to get just the outcome we want. We work as hard as we can to give ourselves and others exactly what is needed. But even when we do everything exactly right, things still don't turn out as we planned. The result often isn't just unwanted but also painful and unjust. It shakes the faith we have in the world and in people.

In short, sometimes bad things happen to good people. Sometimes we are being the very best people we can be and bad things happen to us. We must accept this reality if we wish to find physical, mental, and emotional balance. We can't manipulate or control every outcome. We must develop an attitude of acceptance toward each and every situation in our lives, always working for the good of ourselves and others, but at the same time letting go of the things we cannot change. This is the path of a bodhisattva.

Going beyond treating the emotions as friends and enemies is no small task. It is part of the lifelong practice of the Buddhist path. As practitioners of this path, we will be challenged in the way we relate to our emotions. Rather than diving into our emotions, or avoiding them, we will be called upon to let them go, first at crucial moments and then at every moment. Letting go does not mean trying to force them to disappear. It does not mean pretending we are "beyond" them—that is, emotional distancing. It is the ability, in the moment, to completely free ourselves from their grip. Letting go of the emotions is the Buddhist answer to going beyond the dichotomy of indulging and avoiding. But, ironically, mastering the art of letting go of the emotions will take all the courage and strength we have. When we reflect on the example of Patrul Rinpoche's life as a wandering beggar, we may or may not feel inspired. We may not think it takes so much courage to cast off the comforts of the world and wander as he did. But his example is symbolic of the incredible amount of courage it takes to not put energy into the ordinary ways of the world that cause so much suffering to everyone around us, yet to still care about the world deeply. It takes great courage to let go of ordinary emotions and to relate to others in a way that has the potential to bring compassion and wisdom to every connection.

Some of us might feel apprehensive about this fresh approach. It means that we are fully responsible for dealing with our emotions and our emotional reactions at each and every moment. It means we can't blame others for making us unhappy, because we know that we have the power to transform our own emotional experience ourselves. We are going to have to let go of the importance we place on the events, good and bad, in the past to which we attribute a lot of meaning, so that we are free to be flexible and open in the present. But in doing so we will find one of the keys to genuine happiness—making our emotions less powerful, less prominent, and less "who we are."

Many of us start out feeling excited to work on our emotional imbalances. But in truth, in our very depths, most of us feel terrified when we hear that we must start focusing less on how we feel. *What if people take advantage of me? What if someone is unkind to me and I don't retaliate? What if I let go of my fears and stop protecting myself, and those fears become reality?* We may have all kinds of anxiety and apprehension about what might happen if we stop holding on to our emotions, and we may not realize how much better we are going to feel if we do. Have we ever wondered what it feels like to be happy, anyway? Happiness, in the context of the Buddhist teachings, is not just another fleeting emotion in contrast to sadness or anger. Happiness is an unconditional state of well-being that is neither knocked down nor buoyed up by external circumstances. It is a way of being that is open, flexible, and capable of meeting whatever arises with joyfulness and appreciation. This true happiness is like an elusive stranger in our lives. We catch it in fleeting glimpses, but as we try to keep it with us, our attachment destroys its very essence.

Tibetans have a saying: "Happiness is hard to bear." Even when something is going well, we may not have the mind stability to enjoy it. We may already be worried about losing it. We may sabotage it. We may not recognize this stranger's face. Whatever your worry, anxiety, or skepticism—hang in there. This journey toward happiness has been taken by many great masters in the past and many spiritual practitioners of this modern age. There are so many ways to start and sustain this long journey, and many of them are described in the pages that follow.

2

Using Lojong to Tame
the Emotions

THE RENOWNED Buddhist master Jowo Je Atisha (982–
1054) was a sage from India known for bringing the extremely pure Kadampa lineage of Buddhism from India to Tibet
nearly one thousand years ago. One thing that made Atisha such
a unique and renowned master is that he took the teachings on
bodhichitta (Skt. awakened mind) as his main and constant practice. As we learn from the example of Atisha's life and practice,
bodhichitta practice can help us become extremely skillful at
working with our emotions. Though *bodhichitta* literally means
"awakened mind," it carries with it the further implication of the
aspiration to place all sentient beings in the state of enlighten-
ment, which indirectly enables us to realize the nature of wisdom
ourselves.

A simpler way that we can understand bodhichitta is that its
very essence is to put the well-being and happiness of others before our own, as we discussed in the previous chapter. Many of
us may think we already do this. If we think in this manner, we
probably need to dig deeper. Even though Western culture has
a long tradition of practicing compassion, it can still be difficult
to get a sense of what it means to train in bodhichitta, which
goes far beyond ordinary compassion. We can distinguish the

practice of bodhichitta from more ordinary empathy and compassion because with bodhichitta, we are trying to unearth the deepest layers of self-centeredness that lie buried within us in connection to our positive action. The wish to get something for ourselves can have many faces. It is also intrinsically related to our emotional state of mind and self-attachment. When we help others, we may have more overt wishes for those people to return the favors in kind. But we also probably have other, more hidden selfish motivations, such as avoiding uncomfortable situations, being self-protective, or making ourselves feel more secure, using our positive actions to feel good about ourselves or making others like us or think about us in certain ways. We should also remember that the benefit to ourselves, the realization of wisdom that results from the perfection of bodhichitta, is an indirect result. If we were to act kindly and selflessly toward others while having the wish to attain some kind of spiritual goal, we would not be practicing genuine bodhichitta.

We may not think of seemingly positive actions as being the manipulators of our life situations, but when we entertain selfish thoughts and feelings, we are always, directly or indirectly, trying to be the architects of the scenarios we are facing. When we start to train seriously in bodhichitta, we begin to reverse our ordinary selfish tendencies—the same unhappy tendencies that cause us to keep the focus on ourselves and our own emotions. So it follows that to start training in bodhichitta, we must be willing to turn our ordinary ways of thinking, feeling, and doing upside down.

Bodhichitta is not a practice easily mastered because the emotional habits that we have developed run so deep. They are not like the ordinary paths worn into a hillside by frequent walking but rather more like deep ravines cut by swift flowing water. In fact, it is said that of all the teachings in Tibetan Buddhism, the teachings on bodhichitta are the most difficult to master because this practice fundamentally transforms the ordinary approach we take toward every aspect of our lives.

The difficulty of practicing bodhichitta in the modern world was in fact prophesied by the Tibetan masters of old. Traditionally the teachings on bodhichitta were always the first teachings to be received, practiced, and mastered, but that isn't so in the modern world. It was said that in this modern age, the teachings of bodhichitta would become a secret aspect of the dharma, becoming more and more hidden as the years passed. This prophecy refers to the fact that in this modern age, people have extremely strong emotions and strong self-attachment. Fewer and fewer people see the value in releasing the grip they have on their emotions—or rather, that their emotions have on them—or dedicating themselves to spiritual practice. When we have the chance to read about and reflect on bodhichitta, or to begin to put it into practice, we should feel extremely fortunate that we have made a connection with such a genuine approach to spiritual growth and development that is said to be so rare and hard to find in this modern age.

The Approach of Ordinary Beings

In the famous text *The Thirty-Seven Practices of a Bodhisattva*, the Buddhist master Gyalsé Togmé Zangpo (1297–1371) describes the ordinary approach of ordinary beings as treating our friends and loved ones with attachment and love, and treating those we dislike or feel disconnected to with anger, hatred, or distaste. But because bodhichitta is a state of heart and mind that enables us, ultimately, to love others equally and impartially, we are called upon to change this habit we have of relating to our emotions, as well as to our connections, as friends and enemies. When we practice bodhichitta, we must be willing to appreciate, love, and care for all sentient beings despite our perceptions, the history or lack of history between us, or our current relationships with them. What is even more difficult is that we must be willing to put aside our own needs, comfort, and wishes in order to make space in our hearts and minds for others and their needs.

Atisha and the Lojong Teachings

Like Patrul Rinpoche and other sages, Atisha had a radical approach to living. When we view his life through the lens of bodhichitta, we see that he exemplifies the way to heal ourselves physically, mentally, and emotionally so that we are healthy enough to serve others. It is said that when Atisha traveled to Tibet to teach the dharma, he brought with him a monkey who constantly soiled his body and his clothing, and an irate cook who often shouted at him. Because Atisha was a great Indian Buddhist master, he was highly revered and respected by all Tibetan people. He could have had the most comfortable home and the best clothing, and he could have been treated like a king by everyone around him. But Atisha, being wise, knew this would not ultimately bring him happiness or enable him to serve others. When asked by his students why he didn't just get rid of the annoyances of the monkey and the cook, Atisha said, "All of you Tibetans are so nice to me. How will I ever learn to practice patience if I don't live with the monkey and the cook? You see the monkey and the cook as enemies. Actually, they show me more kindness than my students do by giving me the opportunity to practice."

In this story, Atisha gives us even more insight into the nature of friends and enemies. According to Atisha and the general Mahayana Buddhist teachings, the greatest kindnesses are given to us by those things—or people—that we want to get rid of, those things that make us uncomfortable, angry, irritated, and impatient. And the kindnesses shown by those who love and treat us well are more like the actions of enemies, since these kindnesses reinforce our sense of self-cherishing, which only brings us greater and greater unhappiness.

This story about the life and habits of Atisha is a beautiful introduction to the canon of teachings referred to as *lojong*, literally "mind training," practiced by all followers of the bodhisattva path. In the West, lojong has come to be associated with a set of slogans and sayings that help us kindle mindfulness in many different situations. But in the context of the Buddhist tradition, lojong is a vast topic. We could think of it as the whole of engaged spiritual practice, using all the situations we face—positive, negative, and neutral—for self-improvement and spiritual development. So lojong cannot be limited to one practice or set of teachings. Actually, all of the eighty-four thousand different teachings taught by the historical Buddha Shakyamuni can be called lojong; their goal is to help us decrease and ultimately destroy self-attachment.

Because he was a great lojong master, Atisha can be considered an authoritative source of advice about how to develop emotional balance and stability. After all, Atisha was willing to approach life in a way that tore down all the walls and boundaries in his mind, so that he could get beyond his ordinary habits and simply work for the happiness and welfare of others. We may think that someone living a thousand years ago couldn't comprehend the kinds of difficulties we face in the modern world today. But no matter what our problems and difficulties, the root of our unhappiness is exactly the same: we cannot get what we want, and unwanted things keep happening. We have taken birth and now are facing the aging, sickness, and death of ourselves and our loved ones.

How do we get beyond being stuck in the wish for things to be just as we want them to be? The great master Atisha gives three pieces of advice that help us begin walking the path of lojong. If we work through these three pieces of advice in order, we will begin to gain more insight into our emotional state of mind and how we can go about causing a real transformation to happen within us.

First, Reflect on Selflessness

Atisha's teachings tell us first to train in understanding, intellectually and emotionally, the nature of "selflessness." The word *selflessness* was coined in English to describe a state that is the opposite of self-attachment. Selflessness is the dharma's way of saying that nothing in this world is real. Here, the word *real* is defined by the dharma to mean "permanent and unchanging." We may think we understand that the world around us and everything in it, including ourselves, is changing, but it is our innate habit to attribute a sense of reality to the world and ourselves. That is to say, we emotionally believe, or stubbornly insist on pretending, that everything is going to continue on just as it is now. Sometimes we persist in pretending, even when we see the error in our thinking. Our habit is that strong.

The selflessness that Buddhism describes is twofold. First, there is the selflessness of the individual. We individual beings are said to be selfless because we lack a lasting, unchanging, and permanent self. We are attached to our bodies, minds, and emotions, and so we identify with them as being aspects of a permanent, real self. Even though this is our emotional habit, we all know that this self that we cherish so much changes year by year, month by month, day by day, and moment by moment. The second type of selflessness is called *the selflessness of phenomena*. This means that we relate to our perceptions, emotions, sensory experiences, people, and places in this world in just the same way as we relate to our own bodies. In other words, we extend this sense of a permanent "I" to everything around us, and so we grasp on to our perceptions, emotions, and experiences as though they're real.

When we emotionally invest in this view and perception of the world around us, we develop hopes, fears, and expectations of how things are supposed to be. We build up ideas about how our lives should go, how people should treat us, what we should experience, what we deserve, what kinds of suffering we shouldn't have to experience, and so on. If we think about the fact that neither us nor the outside world are fixed, we come to see that our thoughts, perceptions, and emotions are all based on a big mistake. In Buddhism, this big mistake we are all making is the ultimate cause of suffering; it is called *ignorance*. Ignorance describes a state of mind that is dull and dark, because with ignorance we cannot see that we are causing our own turmoil and distress by trying to make ourselves and the world something other than they are. It would make sense, then, that if we could relax the grip we have on ourselves, as well as on the outside world, our emotional reactions to the world around us would be less intense, less visceral. It follows that in order to relate to our emotions in a more balanced way, we will have to deeply contemplate the teachings on impermanence and apply them as lojong.

Next, Focus on Training the Mind

Atisha teaches that "the supreme kind of taming is to tame the mind." What this means is that the fundamental change that needs to happen in all of us must come from within. Many of us put a lot of energy into influencing how we appear and sound to others on the outside. For example, we may feel deeply upset or wounded inside, or maybe numb or indifferent, but we want to appear to others as if everything is just right, so we focus a lot of energy on how we look and what we say. Although it may be skillful and help us achieve harmony with others when we pull ourselves together in this way, this doesn't help us achieve overall emotional balance. After all, even a cat can walk mindfully with soft footfalls, seeming completely calm and undisturbed despite a loud clamor in the room. Likewise, if we have read many books or attended many dharma teachings, we can also talk to others in a way that makes us seem knowledgeable about spirituality. We can seem like genuine practitioners, and others may see us that way. But just because words have penetrated our brains doesn't mean they have been internalized by our hearts and minds. We may even be able to talk about Buddhist ideas such as selflessness and decreasing self-attachment without applying those teachings to ourselves at all. After all, even a parrot can repeat what it hears. If we have not really worked on taming the mind, sooner or later our weaknesses will come through.

The worst part of this sort of noninternalization of the teachings is that our efforts will come to naught. The goal of lojong practice is to help us relax so that we can open up to a new way of thinking, feeling, and doing. The result of lojong practice is to find contentment with ourselves and the many positive, negative, and neutral situations we face throughout our lives. But if we don't begin to break down the mind's ordinary tendency to put our own comfort and wishes first, our personalities will not be tamed and transformed by the practice of lojong. When we force ourselves to appear differently on the outside than we feel on the inside, this can be very painful. We're split in two—still experiencing the same painful emotional patterns as before, but straining to appear as though we are beyond those patterns. Intimacy with ourselves and others is difficult to achieve when we are divided into pieces. And, others may not realize how much we are hiding. We might be able to keep up a charade for months or even years, but eventually either we will be exhausted by our own efforts or the charade will fall apart on its own. Patrul Rinpoche calls this "pretending to practice the dharma" as opposed to "practicing the dharma as dharma."

Buddhism is a spiritual path that helps us bring our inside feelings and our outside appearance into harmony. If we rely upon the practice of bodhichitta to help us open up to others and widen the net of our love and compassion beyond where it is now, then the outer expression of this emotional opening will also be genuine. And if the heart and mind relax within us, the outer expression of that also puts others at ease and brings greater or more genuine intimacy to all our connections.

There is a famous story from the life of the Buddha Shakyamuni on the importance of taming the mind. There was once a king who told his elephant tamer to tame a young elephant for the king to ride. Of course, the elephant tamer was quite skillful, and in time he was able to tame the elephant to do anything he wanted. The king was pleased and asked the tamer to showcase the elephant's skills. Even if the elephant tamer commanded the elephant to pick up a red-hot iron with its trunk, the elephant would obediently follow his command. After seeing the show of the elephant's skills, the king requested that the elephant be decorated with gold and ribbons so he could ride the elephant while sightseeing.

As the king was riding the elephant down the road, it suddenly caught the scent of a female elephant and charged after it. Holding on for his life, the king shouted angrily at the elephant tamer, "I thought you said this elephant had been tamed!"

The elephant tamer calmly replied, "It's true that I tamed the elephant, but I only have the method to tame the elephant's body, not its mind."

The king thought for a moment, then he asked, "What do you mean by taming the mind? Is there anyone who can really do that?" The elephant tamer told him about the Buddha Shakyamuni, a spiritual master who knew how to completely purify and transform the mind's emotions and habits. It is said that upon hearing these words about the Buddha, the king became a practitioner of the dharma and a devoted follower.

As this story illustrates, if we do not tame the mind—meaning, if we do not fundamentally change the mind's selfish habits—there is no way we can reach the realization of spiritual masters, or even attain ordinary peacefulness and contentment. Why is that?

The strongest habit we have is acting selfishly, and we have acted on this habit since the moment we were born. We were born screaming, needing care and attention, without any thought of others. Even though we may have grown into the ability to focus on ourselves less and to care for others more, we followed this same basic pattern. Not only that, but our culture, society, history, parents, loved ones, and friends have been encouraging us to be selfish all along. They have been exemplifying, teaching, and modeling this behavior, because we tend to believe that this way of thinking and acting will help us feel happier and suffer less. Nearly everything and everyone in the world around us make it difficult for us to give up this basic habit of putting ourselves first, and they assist us in making our self-attachment strong and rigid. But the great sages such as Shakyamuni, Shantideva, Atisha, Gyalsé Togmé Zangpo, Patrul Rinpoche, Jigme Lingpa, and great modern masters such as our root lama, Tsara Dharmakirti Rinpoche, realized the real problem lies in the way that we ordinary beings think. The way we put ourselves in the center and then treat the rest of the world as friends or enemies causes us to be extremely unhappy.

There are a few main problems we run into when we want to begin to train the mind in bodhichitta, and change our fundamental way of thinking about ourselves, our emotions, and other beings. First, we must get past our skepticism. It is difficult, and perhaps frightening, to believe that focusing less on ourselves and our emotions will help us feel better. We all probably have our own reasons why we focus on our feelings and way of thinking so much. For one thing—they're *ours*, and the attachment we have to them is deep and intrinsic. But also, in many cases, it can seem as if paying attention to our feelings helps us resolve them so that we will feel better. So we focus inward. We dialogue and reason with ourselves. We try to understand our own feelings. We try to figure out what it was that we wanted to happen and what would have made us feel better at the time—or what we think will make us feel better now. We fantasize that if things had only gone that way, we would feel better now.

But we should reflect on what has happened during our lifetimes so far in this regard. Armed with that evidence, we should honestly ask ourselves if focusing on our emotions has ever really made us feel better. Perhaps it has in some ways. We may feel justified in our feelings, or we may have been able to let go of a certain amount of our past resentments, grievances, or desires. But in many cases the emotions and wounds remain either on or just below the surface. We continue to react to them as though the painful situations that we have been trying to work through are still happening right now.

There are other difficulties that surface when we try to pacify the emotions by keeping our focus on them. This way of handling the emotions also takes an incredible amount of time and energy. Oftentimes when we focus intensively on our emotions we become physically imbalanced, and the result is that we become sick or exhausted. We may have difficulty fulfilling the duties of ordinary life, such as completing tasks at school or at work. Or our energy may become heavy and low from keeping the focus on our mental unhappiness, and we may feel too tired to do ordinary things such as cook or clean up the house. We may put our health at risk and leave our minds in disarray.

Focusing too much on our emotions can also cause negative consequences in our close relationships. Sometimes we may be so focused inward that we lose touch with others. We may feel incapable of offering them support during times of trouble, or perhaps we are so wrapped up in ourselves that we do not even realize when others are struggling with difficulties themselves. Also, when we are wholly focused on ourselves, we may miss the chance to do something positive to benefit our families, communities, or the greater society. On top of all of this, focusing on our emotions doesn't bring the same kind of acceptance, peace of mind, and sense of relaxation that spiritual practice does.

Taking the Plunge

If we really wish to enact meaningful change, we'll have to take the plunge and start taking the focus off our emotions. We will have to see what happens if we choose to focus less on particular emotions or particular states of mind. For example, we could choose to let go of an emotion—or put less energy into it—instead, following Atisha's advice to focus on the quality of the mind. We could begin to notice how we are being self-centered or self-cherishing, and where our own hopes, fears, and expectations are causing us unhappiness. It can be difficult to find the willingness to drop old patterns and try something new. But in this case, we can feel free to experiment. We can gradually apply the lojong teachings to the mind and examine the results of our experimentation. There aren't many people willing to adopt a whole new way of thinking, feeling, and doing without first going through a period of experimentation and examination. We can support our spiritual practice, making it strong and stable, by being willing to use fresh techniques to resolve old, habitual difficulties.

But even if we cross this hurdle of believing that this experiment might work, the emotional habits we have developed won't be changed quickly or easily. In order to be effective, the lojong teachings must be applied over a long period of time and applied consistently. We must be willing to apply them in intense, emotionally charged situations as well as in ordinary situations for us to begin to change our habits and thought patterns. It is difficult to apply the lojong teachings in either case. First, in emotionally charged situations we may be too fearful or too invested in our emotions to loosen our grip and try another approach. Second, in ordinary situations we might downplay the need for change and not make the effort to apply the teachings. Finally, even if we begin to apply the lojong teachings and make noticeable changes in ourselves, we will probably start to notice resistance.

Resistance may come from the outside, as the people in our lives resist changes in us and act in ways meant to cause us to change back to how we used to be. But resistance also comes from the inside. We resist changes in ourselves because we do not want to face fear and uncertainty about how things will unfold in the future due to the changes we are making right now.

Third, Focus on Your Motivation

A final piece of advice that Atisha gives is to make the motivation paramount at all times. The motivation he is talking about is what we call an "excellent motivation," and it means having a deep wish to benefit others. Such motivation may be fairly easy to give rise to in given moments but is very hard to develop consistently. In order to become an embodiment of this kind of excellent motivation, we need to let go of our old way of thinking. After all, our ordinary way of thinking, feeling, and doing is contaminated by thoughts of ourselves and full of self-cherishing. Even when we wish to do something good for others, if we look closely we will likely find at least a small shred of self-interest. It is extremely difficult to find a situation where we have acted 100 percent for another's welfare, without any thought to ourselves. So again, in the context of lojong, a pure and altruistic motivation needs to be generated again and again, once we notice it waning or becoming corrupted in some way.

Atisha gives these three pieces of advice regarding the practice of lojong in this order because the latter rely upon the former. For example, unless we understand selflessness, we will not be willing or able to tame the mind. And without taming the mind, we will not be able to train in an excellent motivation. So we should take up these three pieces of advice together, allowing them to complement one another as they also help us develop our lojong practice.

Finally, we should realize that lojong practice is neither easy to do nor easily achieved. However, it is extremely rewarding. After many years of practice, we begin to find that situations and emotions that used to baffle us or tie up our energy completely are easily resolved. We can relax and breathe even when we are facing difficulties. But when we first begin to practice, we should realize that our sense of self is as hard as granite. Our emotions are a massive part of our sense of self. We know who we are because of how we feel. And often we are afraid to let go of how we feel for fear of losing ourselves. Think of the hardness of granite. Even if it's rained on for one hundred years, the shape of a granite mountain peak will not change perceptibly. The self-attachment, ego, and identity that we believe in is just like this. This imagery can help us to understand why the advice of these great bodhisattva masters is so emphatic and radical.

Lojong, or mind training, is just like using a chisel to chip away at our hard edges and destroy our painful habits. The end result is a softer, more flexible version of who we thought we were. So the next time we encounter an irritating monkey or an irate chef, we may think twice about how we treat them. Are they really our enemy or are they actually the one giving us the opportunity to change?

3

Working with Grasping
toward the Emotions

I F   W E   H A V E   B E G U N to put some of Atisha's lojong teachings into practice, we have probably started to taste the deep
resistance we all have toward change—especially when it means
giving up our ideas, habits, emotions, or anything else we think
we need to feel okay. We have a formidable task ahead of us:
giving up cherishing our egos and the identities we've developed
over the course of our lives isn't easy.

In the West, some of us may feel confused about this idea of
"self-cherishing" as it is presented in the dharma. It may seem
as though only people who love themselves, or have strong self-
esteem, are self-cherishing. If we dislike ourselves, if we experience feelings of self-hatred, we must not have self-cherishing
or self-attachment, right? But this is a misunderstanding of
self-cherishing.

Self-cherishing is a term that describes the relationship we
have toward our emotions, our perceptions, our bodies, and our
thoughts. No matter whether we like ourselves or hate ourselves,
we relate to the world based on our own perceptions, seeing
through the lens created by the collection of thoughts and experiences we have had in our lives. So we could more accurately
describe self-cherishing as grasping at our own point of view.

The truth is that we all cherish our own point of view simply because it is *ours*.

We might think that if we see ourselves as low and miserable people, unworthy of the lives and talents we have and the people who love us, that we are not self-cherishing. But in fact, from the point of view of the Buddhist teachings, thinking this way is no different than believing that we deserve better or are more worthy than others. Whenever we choose to grasp at strong beliefs about who we are and side with these beliefs over everything else, we are engaging in self-cherishing.

Because self-hatred is a point of view or way of thinking that we grasp at, it is also a form of self-cherishing. It may seem ironic to use the word *cherish* in connection with emotions such as self-deprecation or self-loathing, but *cherish* refers to a kind of love that is a deep, innate self-identification. Because we identify with our bodies and minds as *who we are*, we cannot escape the net of self-cherishing.

For those of us who dance the dance of self-hatred, we tend to do it in all our life situations. The self-cherishing of self-hatred has so many faces and appears in so many different ways that it is very hard to recognize that self-hatred underlies many of the unhealthy behaviors we have. For example, we may act out self-hatred in our ordinary relationships by sabotaging healthy connections when we feel undeserving, or by withdrawing and isolating ourselves from others when we lack the energy and confidence to connect. We may engage in unhealthy eating and sleeping patterns, or avoid paying attention to daily needs that help keep us physically, mentally, and emotionally stable. We may engage in behavior that is dangerous to ourselves and others, such as driving too fast or recklessly, or not attending to our bodies when we are sick or injured. In all these cases, it seems that we dislike and disregard ourselves. On one level, this is true. We are acting in contradiction to our own self-interest. But we should also understand that our deep identification with ourselves, our innate cherishing of the idea of ourselves as "bad" or undeserving people, is the true cause of this destructive behavior.

Not only do we act in self-defeating ways in our ordinary lives, but we also bring this tendency into our spiritual practice. For example, if our dharma teachers see us as worthy and capable students but we are obsessed with the idea that we can't possibly be—we are too miserable or too stupid to learn, or we've done too many bad things to deserve this kindness—we are self-cherishing. We may also sabotage the connections we have with our spiritual communities in various ways. If we attend a meditation group, we may project our feelings of difference or unworthiness upon those around us, thinking that they dislike us or that we are unlikable. As a result, we may emotionally separate ourselves from the group. Over time, that emotional separation manifests as disconnection and may cause us to leave the group. However, when the time comes to leave, it will probably seem like just another time that we couldn't fit in with others. We may not realize we had any part in what happened.

Seen through this lens, the emotion of self-hatred is very strange indeed. By simply following the pattern of disliking or hating ourselves, we reinforce our strong sense of self, which makes us so miserable. Self-hatred simply adds fuel to the fire. It's important to see the deep sense of confusion caused by our self-cherishing. When we express self-hatred, we are actually expressing hatred and attachment toward ourselves simultaneously! By feeding the emotion of self-hatred, we persist in putting ourselves in the center of everything—the ultimate sign of self-attachment.

The emotion of self-hatred is destructive in a variety of ways, some more obvious than others. Most obviously, self-hatred puts us in a state of mind in which we feel incapable or unworthy of love and transformation. But also, feeding the emotion of self-hatred is like adding brick and mortar to identities that already bring us incredible amounts of unhappiness. We are filling in all the cracks, and making our identification with difficult emotions such as depression, helplessness, or hopelessness more solid and real.

That is why it can be said that self-cherishing occurs in spite of whatever attitudes, feelings, or perceptions we have of ourselves. Whether we feel positively or negatively toward ourselves, deserving or undeserving, worthy or unworthy, we all grasp and cherish the ideas we have. We all focus heavily on ourselves, our own ways of thinking, our perceptions, and our emotions. Our investment in these thoughts and emotions makes them seem justifiable and important because they are part of our sense of self. Therefore, according to the dharma, our friends or enemies themselves don't bring us unhappiness but rather unhappiness comes from our insistence on placing others in those categories so that we can more firmly reinforce *who we think we are*.

The Purpose of Identity

Why do we do this? Why do we hold on to this sense of self when it is the source of our suffering? For starters, our identities tend to make us feel safe. Even if we identify as being miserable, tormented beings, at least we know who we are and we don't have to venture much outside of that. We can keep our world intact. We know how to function within that. We know where everyone and everything fits and we have the script for how to relate to them. Shaking up this sense of self can be very unsettling, even threatening, but it is the key to meeting our lives with greater skill, openness, and clarity.

Some of us may have come to a point where we realize that self-cherishing is what causes us suffering. Because we are resourceful, we may try to use ordinary methods to cut through it. But how do we get rid of such a destructive pattern? Because we know that self-cherishing is a formidable enemy, we may try to use a method that is equally destructive or harsh. In other words, we may use another rigid and painful emotional pattern to try to correct the pain-inducing pattern we already have. Self-judgment—as well as judging others—is something that we might try to use to cut through our self-cherishing. For example, we may berate ourselves for having the emotions, thoughts, and perceptions that we have. But even the intense energy and emotion of judgment cannot cut through self-cherishing. Expressing this judgment toward ourselves simply adds another layer of unhappiness on top of the feelings we already experience. It does nothing to release the painful emotion that was the source of our initial reaction.

Self-cherishing cannot be decreased using our ordinary habits and ordinary ways of thinking. We need a way to get to the root of the matter—a spiritual technique such as lojong. Ordinary methods work only on the surface. But self-cherishing is a deep and ingrained habit. We must apply a strong method to turn it on its head and release ourselves from its grip.

Buddhism teaches that our ordinary worldly ways—treating loved ones as friends and those we dislike as enemies—are based on the dull and dark state of mind called ignorance. When we follow the ways of worldly beings, we are always caught in the trap of self-cherishing. We blindly pursue happiness and avoid suffering in any way that we can. However, we should be aware that if we have the courage to do so, we can transform this whole way of thinking. All the rules of the game of life can be dropped in an instant. If we are more open and flexible, and have the courageous mind of a bodhisattva as Patrul Rinpoche did, we will realize that we can survive without self-cherishing. *It is possible.* The lives of the great spiritual masters of Buddhism as well as other spiritual traditions show that it is not just possible to live with less self-interest and self-cherishing, but that we can live more happily, with more contentment and peace of mind. This is because genuine joy and happiness are born from connection with others and from working for others' happiness over one's own.

That is why spiritual masters are so awe-inspiring. They have understood that losing self-cherishing is the key to peace and contentment. But they have also understood that the best methods to lose this self-cherishing are gradual and gentle, albeit radical in comparison to the way that we ordinary beings think.

The Roots of Self-Cherishing

The main conditions for self-cherishing are twofold. First, there is the incredible attachment we have toward our emotional experience, which is composed of our thought patterns, perceptions, and reactions to sensory experience. Second, we engage in an intense identification with the form of the physical body as well as the forms of objects, places, and people in our environment. Collectively, these make up what is called the *mara* of form (Skt. *skandamara*). This chapter will deal only with the self-cherishing and attachment we have to our emotional experience, while attachment to the form of the physical body will be explored in the next chapter.

In the Buddhist teachings, *mara* is a word that describes a spiritual obstacle, or more literally, a spiritual demon. We are free to attribute meaning to this concept as literally or symbolically as we like. In the traditional Buddhist teachings, maras are sometimes depicted as harmful beings or tempting spirits. But we can also understand maras as our inner shadow sides. It is the incredibly powerful energy that is the summation of our negative habits and accumulated karma. When these maras show their faces—when we have to face our shadow sides—we may feel as upset or unstable as though we had seen actual demons. But not to worry. All the inner workings of our hearts and minds can be understood and digested gradually by us, as we begin to wake up through spiritual practice.

Sensitivity as an Expression of Self-Cherishing

We can name the attachment we have toward our emotional experience as "sensitivity." *Sensitive* is a word that can sometimes be laden with judgment or that can be spoken as a criticism. We may say that others are too sensitive if we feel they are out of balance or too emotional. We also may feel that sensitivity causes others to take our words or actions too seriously, resulting in conflicts or hard feelings. But sensitivity is not an inherently bad trait. The positive side of sensitivity can be that it generates a source of connection and closeness. However, as we may also have experienced, when it's imbalanced, sensitivity can be a tremendous source of instability and unhappiness, causing divisions and misunderstandings in our relationships.

The word *sensitive* can be examined in the context of both the English and Tibetan languages; the contrast between how these two languages and associated cultural systems understand this word offers insight into its positive and negative aspects. In English, the word *sensitive* can mean "quick to respond to slight changes or influences." This definition brings out the more positive aspect of sensitivity. For example, seen this way sensitivity is a trait that can make it easier to empathize with others, to be more readily able to respond to their needs. Because sensitive people are more subtly connected with their own experience, they can also more easily understand how others feel and what they may be experiencing. Sensitivity can be a special kind of intelligence. It can help us understand and respond to situations and others skillfully because it causes us to be so in tune with what is going on. These aspects of sensitivity should not be abandoned. They should be nurtured by our spiritual practice, as they help us develop compassion and bodhichitta.

The Tibetan language defines the word *sensitivity* differently. According to Tibetan etymology, the word *sensitive* (Tib. *tshor sla bo*) means "easily emotional." This definition points to the uglier, more destructive side of sensitivity. When we become strongly reactive to our inner experience, we become too emotional too easily. This results in emotional imbalance and turbulence, and lots of ups and downs. We can become intensely attached to how we *want* to feel versus what is happening at the moment. This can create an overall lack of tolerance for unwanted experiences and emotions. We may want to control ourselves, others, or our environment in order to avoid certain experiences or feelings. Although a balanced or healthy sense of sensitivity can help us connect with others, being too sensitive can cause us to disconnect and withdraw as we try to shut out unwanted experiences.

When we place too great a focus on our internal experience, we naturally increase and solidify our sense of self-cherishing. Again, whether we like the experience or dislike it, whether we feel worthy or unworthy, we are still placing ourselves and our experience in the center of everything. We identify with it, making it solid and real. We place an extremely strong focus upon our inner world. We come to believe that we *are* what we experience — that we *are* what we feel.

Using Lojong to Look in the Mirror

One of the reasons that our emotions affect us so much is that rather than using them as sources of information, we instantly identify with them. No matter what is arising inside of us, we immediately attend to it. We may do this in different ways. Our immediate identification with the emotions may weigh us down, or cloud the mind so that we have difficulty communicating or thinking clearly. We may react with feelings of volatility that cause us to act or speak impulsively, lashing out at whoever is nearby or whoever we feel close to. Or we may seem not to have any response at all. A sense of coldness or distance may come over the heart and mind. Even though we do not appear to be having an emotional response, we are still completely occupied by the experience of the emotions.

In all these cases, our identification with the emotions influences our thoughts and perceptions. It is as though we are wearing emotional glasses; our emotional identification influences the very way that we see, as if we are nearsighted. The ironic part is that we usually can't see ourselves at all. We are so focused on the people and situations around us, and so invested in our emotional responses, that we fail to see who we are and how we actually behave and treat others. It is often the case that how we see ourselves is completely different from how others see and experience us. This can be a great source of misunderstanding and conflict in our relationships. We may mean to be kind, but don't realize that we are acting in ways that hurt or upset others. On the one hand, we need not try to control how others perceive us. This is not something we are capable of doing. But on the other hand, we can try to express on the outside the intentions that we have on the inside. Especially, as blossoming bodhisattvas, we can try to show on the outside all the positive wishes for others and good qualities that we have inside of us.

When we fail to have an accurate sense of ourselves and our own emotional responses—both our strengths and weaknesses—we are not in a good position to make effective change. Changing our emotional patterns requires us to be aware of the patterns that we have, especially those patterns that seem to control the majority of our energy and affect our close relationships. Simply following our emotional patterns or reflecting on past experiences won't give us this kind of insight.

When we use the approach of lojong, we approach the emotions as a source of information rather than as what shapes our responses and behavior. For example, if we hear or see something that makes us angry, we attempt to recognize our response of anger as quickly as possible. As soon as we have recognized that we are angry, we reflect on what about the situation caused us to react in anger. When we work with Buddhist mind training, our goal is not to blame outside people or situations for how we feel. Instead we focus on our own responses, negative habits, and self-centeredness. When we notice ourselves having strong emotional responses, we can apply this phrase: "Rather than looking to others, look in the mirror."

This phrase reminds us that we are the source of our own unhappiness, because the root of all unhappiness is self-cherishing. As we reflect on why we have become angry, instead of focusing on what others have done to make us angry, we can instead try to notice what kinds of hopes, fears, or expectations we had toward the situation. For example, if we become angry when someone criticizes us, saying that we have done something wrong that harmed another, if we look in the mirror rather than looking to blame the other person we will likely see that we had some kind of expectation that wasn't met. Often due to our self-cherishing, anger may cause us to feel that we haven't been treated in the manner we deserve. We may also feel that the other person was overly critical, or that what the other person said was flat-out untrue.

Rather than focusing our anger or indignation on the other person, we could instead notice what it was that we wanted from the interaction. We may have wished to be praised rather than criticized. We may have wished the other person understood us better, so they wouldn't have treated us in a way that we didn't like. In this case, we can notice the strong attachment we have to our own good name and good face, and how important it is to us that others like us and think well of us.

We can use the technique of looking in the mirror any time a strong emotion comes up. The Buddhist teachings present the five root emotions—or poisons, so-called because of their poisonous nature—as anger, attachment/desire, jealousy, arrogance, and ignorance. It is likely that whenever we are having strong emotional responses, our responses are related to one of these poisonous emotions. When we apply this lojong technique, our own patterns and emotional responses become a great source of information. We can use the phrase "looking in the mirror," quite literally, to see ourselves more accurately, with all our strengths and weaknesses clearly appearing before us just like seeing our own faces in a mirror. Armed with this information, we will slowly see opportunities for change, or times when we can change our habitual responses and act in ways that are more skillful and less self-centered.

It is likely that we will find it difficult to look in the mirror all the time. We need to be patient with ourselves. When we begin to notice our own emotional responses and see the depth of our attachment to being treated well and respected by others, to have what we want when we want it, and to having things turn out as we plan, we will likely feel discouraged. But remember that a bodhisattva is a hero with endless courage. We can remember the example of Patrul Rinpoche, who had the courage to take on the appearance of a beggar and did not seek the respect, admiration, or praise of anyone. This example can serve as our inspiration to be willing to keep seeing our strengths and weaknesses and, over time, begin to see how others see and experience us rather than how we see ourselves.

The Transcendental Quality of Patience

According to the bodhisattva teachings, the suffering we experience as a reaction to unwanted experiences is based on impatience. We want whatever unpleasantness that is happening to stop—*now*. The root of impatience is anger or intolerance, an expression of one of the five poisons named above. When we develop patience, we not only appease the agitation in our own minds, but we also increase our ability to practice compassion, loving-kindness, and bodhichitta. Why is this?

Bodhichitta enables us to work for others' well-being in any situation. But to skillfully focus on what is best for others, we must be able to lessen the importance of our own thinking and feelings. We must lose the emotionally reactive side of our sensitivity. Otherwise we can't really make room for others. Although we might think we have a good impulse to help, we end up merely trying to shape people in a way that will make them more agreeable to us. The very beginning of bodhisattva activity, what we do as baby bodhisattvas, is to stop reinforcing our preferences and make an effort to be a person who has fewer likes and dislikes.

No matter in what situations we find ourselves, when we don't have so many opinions and preferences we naturally experience more peace of mind. We feel more agreeable, more comfortable, and more able to fit in with others. When we are more tolerant, not only do our minds' stability and experience of meditation improve, but the conduct of our body, speech, and mind also improves because we stop being so reactive. After all, if the great masters weren't transcendentally tolerant and supremely patient, how could a wise master such as Atisha bear to spend his life in the company of an irritating monkey and an irate cook? How could these spiritual masters constantly focus on benefitting others if they were busy worrying about their own likes and dislikes?

There are many stories about the life of Patrul Rinpoche that show his great capacity to practice patience and tolerance. In one story, he by chance entered the home of a wealthy family where a family member had just passed away in order to do a practice to help the deceased through the intermediary states (Tib. *bardo*) after death. Although Patrul Rinpoche was a realized master, strangers rarely recognized him as such. He was overlooked by the family when he arrived, who instead warmly received another lama who was cleaner, well dressed, and accompanied by an attendant. Not only that, but even though Patrul Rinpoche begged for food, the family didn't even offer him a meal. Instead of tea, he was offered some sour water that was skimmed off a batch of fresh cheese—water normally thrown out, as it was unfit to drink.

Because of Patrul Rinpoche's great realization and omniscience, he could see what was in the minds of the others who had come to pray for the deceased. The other lama was wondering what offering he would receive from the family for his service, and a beautiful horse owned by the family had caught his eye. Patrul Rinpoche also saw that the lama's attendant had a very good heart and a genuine wish to help the deceased but that he did not have the spiritual realization to do so.

In the end, despite being disrespected and overlooked, Patrul Rinpoche was the only one who was able to help the deceased transcend the intermediary states. But Patrul Rinpoche, being a master of patience and bodhichitta, did not react in the manner of ordinary people. He did not resent or feel angry about how the family treated him, nor did he feel indignant because he was the one who actually helped their mother. Instead he laughed and made up a verse of poetry expressing the flaws of the ordinary mind and self-cherishing. Having no sense of self-importance or deserving, he delighted in this encounter and his ability to help the deceased, and he wasn't bothered by anything about it at all.

As this story of Patrul Rinpoche's life demonstrates, peace of mind comes when we let go of feelings of criticism and judgment, and especially feelings that we are deserving of certain kinds of treatment. If we really reflect honestly, how many times a day do we feel dissatisfaction or unhappiness because of very small things such as disliking the taste of our lunch, receiving a gift we do not want or need, or hearing unexpected words from another? When we judge and criticize less, when we react less to what we perceive and experience, we become less emotionally involved with what others are saying or doing, and we are not so picky about what exactly is going on. This state is not to be confused with indifference, which is simply another type of emotional response—ignoring what is happening because it doesn't interest us. Ordinarily we lose the opportunity to engage with others mindfully and skillfully because we are preoccupied with our own reactions, feelings, and preferences. When we loosen our grip on our sense of what we deserve, the result is that we are more thoughtful and skillful, and the mind is more even.

Train in Patience as Lojong

No matter what sensory experience we are having at a given moment, our state of mind can always benefit from training in lojong. Earlier we learned to apply the technique of looking in the mirror in order to gain more self-awareness and to understand the intensity of our self-attachment and sensitivity. We also tried to open our eyes to seeing ourselves as others see us rather than as how we see ourselves, to improve our mental and emotional responses, behavior, and connections with others. As we discussed in the previous chapter, we can also apply other lojong techniques, such as cultivating bodhichitta or keeping our minds focused on the happiness of others, in order to put aside many of our unpleasant thoughts and feelings so that our inner reactions are not as strong, painful, and distracting.

Patience is a tool that helps us find peace within ourselves as well as in our families, communities, and the greater society. While the power of patience cannot be understated, the difficulty of practicing patience can also not be understated. In the *Way of a Bodhisattva*, Shantideva says that there is no emotion more destructive than anger, and there is no quality more difficult to master than patience. If we want to achieve patience that can carry us through any emotion, sensitivity, or difficult situation, we must make great effort toward changing our responses, patterns, and habits—the most difficult of all these being the reaction of anger. Shantideva describes anger as an emotion that is like a spark in a haystack—something so destructive that it incinerates everything and everyone in its path, including us. When we are incapable of practicing patience and instead become impatient, angry, or resentful, negative consequences will follow for everyone involved.

As human beings, we tend to be very invested in short-term consequences, forsaking a broader or longer-term view. We most often fail to practice patience because following after our usual responses feels better in the moment. When we try to do something different, we often experience tension both inside of ourselves and in our connections with others, who expect certain kinds of responses from us. But we should always take time to reflect before we act. *What consequence will come from my action? Is that consequence desired or not? Is there a better way to handle the situation to bring a more favorable result, both for myself and for others?* It is almost always true that we can solve a problem, set a boundary, or bring benefit to ourselves and others in a number of ways. It's best to take some time to consider the options and tools that we have so that our words, gestures, behavior, and demeanor are purposeful and skillful rather than rash and inflammatory.

There are pros and cons to expressing an emotion such as anger, but if we take a longer-term view, there are mostly cons. Expressing an emotion such as anger can feel gratifying in the moment. We may feel that we are helping ourselves to set boundaries to be treated with the respect that we deserve. We may feel we are acting rationally in the face of actions or words of others that are simply intolerable. However, no matter the reason for our anger, we still must experience the unhappy result of getting angry ourselves. Expressing the emotion of anger has many consequences that we may not have thought of. Expressing anger causes a great rift in our physical, mental, and emotional energy. Our first instinct may be that expressing anger is a release that makes us feel better. But if we reflect more carefully, we will probably notice that the feeling of release is short lived, and that other negative energy patterns outlive any initial relief we felt. Again, we should reflect on how, in most cases, there is another way of achieving the same result by transforming our angry feelings to skillful action.

Whether or not we express anger probably also depends on the relationships we have with the people with whom we feel conflict. If we are close or intimate with another person, expressing anger may help us clear up misunderstandings and may bring us closer to the other person. On one hand, this can be a sign of trust that the strength of the connection is sufficient to handle our strong emotions. But on the other hand, we can also undermine that trust if we assume that the other person can handle us just as we are, and that we don't have to work on ourselves in our most intimate relationships. Also, if we refuse to let go of our anger after we express it, dragging the conflict on and on, then expressing anger does not bring intimacy. Before we express our thoughts and feelings to others, we should always stop to check in with our motivation. *Am I expressing myself for the good of the relationship? What are my expectations? What compromise do I need to make for the success of the connection?*

It is said that the great, skillful bodhisattvas always have minds filled with love, no matter what they express on the outside. Even if a bodhisattva such as Atisha or Shantideva appeared to be angry, their angry expression served the purpose of benefitting other people or the greater community. Their minds would never be separate from patience, such that they never acted or spoke selfishly or impulsively. They would always give up the short-term benefit for the longer-term view. One aspect of the Vajrayana Buddhist tradition that is often misunderstood is its depictions of wrathful deities and wisdom beings. But this aspect of the Tibetan Buddhist teachings is symbolically making the same point. These sometimes frightful-looking beings are testimony to the fact that even if the appearance of strength or power is needed on the outside, the mind of a realized being is always imbued with love. We need not be afraid of this appearance of strength. However, to be able to embody both compassion and a fierce or strong exterior that can help others when the need arises, we will have to become extremely skillful at working with our own tendency to express anger.

Reflecting on these examples and attempting to apply them to ourselves can be very helpful. For example, we can think about what it would be like to speak to people with the confidence and strength that anger provides but without feelings of heated intensity. We can also reflect on how much it would benefit us to speak from a place that is mentally and emotionally grounded rather than one that is volatile and highly charged. When we reflect in this way, we can see that it is possible to care for ourselves and others without delving into the energy of destructive and intense emotions. We need not be so sensitive, so easily emotional. We simply need to relax, reflect, and take a decisive course of action that keeps others and ourselves in mind.

Apply Lojong by Noticing the Breath

One very simple way of working with anger is paying attention to the breath. For at least a moment, and even longer if you can, notice the rise and fall of the breath. Notice how it feels moving in and out of the body. Notice if heat has risen in the chest, if your energy feels impulsive or out of control. Notice if there are words coming into your mind that you aren't sure you should speak or not. If you aren't sure, try to delay saying anything. Take another deep breath, and allow your energy to settle down.

Applying the bodhisattva path is an extremely effective method for cutting through the intense attachment we have to our emotions. If we can't cut through this self-attachment, we will not escape from the prison of emotional suffering. Therefore, reducing the imbalanced aspect of our sensitivity is an indispensable part of our spiritual practice.

If we reduce the amount of attachment we have to our emotions, not only our dharma activity but also our everyday lives and activities begin to lose their complexity. We don't perceive as many problems and difficulties in our daily lives. We don't react as strongly in the face of minor difficulties. We are more clear-minded, deliberate, and mindful. We become more competent, stable, and able to focus on our own spiritual development.

4

Working with Personal Identity and the Habit of Self-Protection

THE GREAT SPIRITUAL MASTERS of the Buddhist tradition taught that grasping at the body as lasting, permanent, and real is the root of our suffering and unhappiness. In other words, the root of our self-cherishing is in our personal identification with the body as *me*. Because we feel that our very survival is based upon the safety and well-being of the physical body, we develop the habit of being self-protective — that is, defending ourselves. This perceived need to protect ourselves is innate; it is in our blood and goes as deep as the core of our bones. It is part of our animal instinct.

Practitioners of the hard and social sciences generally agree that self-protection is essential. It's a logical way of thinking. After all, if our basic needs aren't met, how can we survive? If we can't fend off the attacks of others, how can we feel safe? But from the perspective of the Buddhist teachings, this animalistic approach only locks us into a cycle of needless suffering. When we examine the effects of severe trauma, we can see the truth of this.

Much of the trauma experienced by human beings stems from the feeling or experience that our ability to protect ourselves has been compromised. If someone we trust, or even a stranger, harms us physically, mentally, or emotionally, in a way that over-whelms us, we will most likely develop an unhealthy response to that experience that impairs our ability to connect with others or ourselves. We may carry an imprint of that experience with us, overlaying it upon the world and the people around us in an attempt to ensure that the experience won't repeat itself. When this happens, it becomes very difficult for us to perceive the present with clarity and to respond accurately to what is happening now. We are caught in an old movie, using the same set of tools we had back then. This can bring considerable confusion to our present lives and those around us who don't understand why we are responding in the ways we are.

The basic technique that many of us rely upon to escape re-living painful experiences is to disconnect, withdraw, ignore, or leave situations that trigger whatever painful patterns or imprints we have developed. Some of us may even dissociate or discon-nect from the physical body. Although this may seem like a kind of negation of our physical selves, it is still a firm expression of self-preservation. Others of us may tend to respond with more volatility or knee-jerk aggression. Maybe on some level we are acting out what behavioral and other kinds of scientists call our fight-or-flight instinct, the body's mechanism for protecting us from mortal danger.

The responses we develop from experiencing trauma are not our fault. We didn't have better tools to deal with it at the time. In Western culture, we place a great emphasis on combing back over traumatic events to determine how, when, and why they oc-curred with the idea that this will help us better understand the pain we are carrying and ultimately free us. To the extent that this kind of examination can help us gain clear insight and unwind unnecessary patterns in our present lives, it may be useful. But this can also lead to a cycle of blame on external circumstances that only amplifies our feelings of helplessness and hopelessness about being able to positively change our present circumstances.

We cannot change what happened to us in the past, but we can respond differently in the present if we are willing to take a different approach.

Trauma is an extreme example that illustrates the depth of our attachment to the physical body. However, we may not all relate to this example. While we may not have experienced trauma, we all have experienced stress at some level. In our culture, stress is also something that we believe to be necessary to some extent. In a more general sense, stress can motivate us or give us the energy to get things done. Its more intense expression can also help save our lives. At the most basic level, physical and emotional stress is a reaction that is meant to keep us safe. When stress begins to build within the body and mind, it triggers the release of adrenaline, causing the acute arousal of the sympathetic nervous system and enabling us to do almost superhuman things in the face of danger or fear. We may be able to make ourselves look tall and big when facing a bear to scare it away, or we may be able to run farther and faster than normal when someone is pursuing us.

We have all likely heard stories that speak to the amazing power of the stress response—such as humans lifting cars off people trapped underneath them. The response of stress serves us by helping us survive. The problem is that when we are overly attached to our physical bodies, and when we perceive the world through the lens of fear that we will face or experience physical harm, the reaction of stress becomes overactive and disconnected from the practicalities of this basic survival instinct. It becomes our normal pattern and normal state of mind, so that we begin to react and experience stress throughout our daily lives. This contributes to our feeling mentally and emotionally unstable, and physically imbalanced, exhausted, or depleted. We may become nervous, anxious, depressed, or sleepless.

Even if we have not experienced trauma or acute stress, we all still feel incredibly attached to our bodies and are willing to protect ourselves at nearly any cost. This intense, protective connection we have toward our physical bodies expresses as self-cherishing and causes us stress when we face unwanted situations or difficulties. Whether it is an acute, magnified response based on past trauma or the more seemingly "normal" response of our animal survival instinct that has been with us since birth and reinforced throughout our lives, the impulse toward self-preservation is essentially the same. This deep habit of self-cherishing begins to extend beyond ordinary physical threats that might challenge or jeopardize our survival, such as someone driving dangerously on the road. It becomes a dominating aspect of our personalities and shapes the emotions that we feel and express. We protect ourselves from comments made about us that we dislike or actions of others that we perceive to be disloyal or not in our personal interest. Even though these things do not physically harm us, still we feel attacked. The overall result is the development of a sensitive and reactive outlook, and an unstable mind. When we have strong reactions to even ordinary situations and sensory experiences, when we cannot ground our minds and emotions, our personal unhappiness and suffering increase.

We can also think about self-protectiveness and our emotional responses in more ordinary terms. *Are they useful? Do they serve me? If so, how?* The approach of many scholars and practitioners of neuroscience, psychotherapy, or other disciplines related to healing the body and mind is to treat the emotions and their expression as serving a useful function that helps us survive. Take the words of a young man who asked the questions, "Doesn't an emotion such as fear serve a great purpose? Doesn't fear protect you in many ways, such as by keeping you from walking out into the middle of a busy street where you will be hit by a car?"

Of course, the answer to these questions is yes. But for a lojong practitioner, there are at least a couple other follow-up questions: Is fear the only emotion that can protect us from the danger of being hit by a car? Is fear the best response to the situation or are we capable of a response that serves us better?

Reflect on the Benefits and Faults of Self-Protection

Is this habit of self-protection a friend or an enemy? Does it keep me safe and increase my well-being, or does it make me miserable, bringing cascades of unpleasant feelings and experiences? If it makes me safe but results in unhappiness or suffering, is this something I want? Or is there another way? We should consider these questions carefully.

Up until now, so much of our life experiences—and the people who love us—have taught us that making ourselves important and protecting ourselves is the very best way to survive. When we stop to consider whether this impulse to protect ourselves is causing us harm, causing our suffering, we may feel incredibly skeptical. Doubts may surface. *What will happen to me if I stop protecting myself? How will I stay out of harm's way? Won't it be more painful if I stop trying to manipulate and plan my life to avoid unwanted experiences?*

It is not wrong to consider these questions. We can use this personal examination and investigation as a way of seeing how willing we are to consider changing some of our own emotional and behavioral patterns. Letting go of self-cherishing, making ourselves and our own comfort less important, and focusing more on the comfort of others—we may never have done these things. Even those of us who consider ourselves to be caretakers, healers, or loving and compassionate friends or family members still protect ourselves by maintaining selfish wishes and ways of thinking. For example, our love and caring may be tinged with wishes to be appreciated, respected, treated well, or taken care of in kind when we need it most. Or we may care for others as a way to avoid our own feelings and assuage our fears—for example, holding on to others to fill our lonely hearts or to occupy ourselves in order to avoid the reality of old age, sickness, and death. We may project our own desires and needs onto others so that we cannot even clearly perceive what is best for them.

Although we may practice ordinary love and compassion in our daily lives, none of us escapes the net of self-cherishing. We can see the truth of this statement because the moment things do not go our way, or people we care for don't recognize our good intentions—perhaps returning our kindness with anger or resentment—we feel hurt and angry. We may not think of these ordinary wishes for love and respect as being self-protective, but even these ordinary, subtle thought patterns bring us great suffering in body and mind when we do not get what we think we deserve or need to feel okay and healthy. Or if we must surrender to letting our loved ones go or not being able to fix their suffering in the ways that we want, we may panic, as if the whole world is dissolving around us. When our own emotions overtake our ability to be simply present and openhearted toward others' suffering, or when we become frustrated because we can't change things for other people that make us uncomfortable, we can be fairly certain that this stems more from our identification with our loved ones as ourselves than it does from true compassion.

Dharma and Self-Protection

The dharma's approach to dealing with life and the emotions contradicts everything we have ever heard. The great masters of the Buddhist tradition, as well as the Buddhist teachings on bodhichitta and lojong, teach us that self-protection is a tendency that needs to be reversed in order to experience genuine happiness. When we really consider what it means to give up the impulse to self-protect, it is almost impossible to even imagine what that would look like, and quite literally how it could be possible to survive without it. The radical approach to living and dealing with the emotions exemplified by masters such as Atisha and Patrul Rinpoche is completely outside of our ordinary ways of thinking. Come back to the question about the usefulness of fear. Great spiritual masters might answer this same question by pointing out that other mental functions can serve the same purpose as fear, without the painful repercussions. For example, well-trained spiritual masters can rely on mindfulness to make sure that they do not step into the paths of moving cars. Also, spiritual masters can rely upon the clarity of their minds to make purposeful decisions. When the mind is clear and relaxed, we are able to see more options and more ways to work skillfully with situations than when we are feeling a highly charged state of mind such as fear.

We can also think more deeply about the nature of fear in an existential way. Perhaps the emotion of fear can keep us safe. However, although it may help protect us from an outer danger, it also brings danger within ourselves, just in a different way. When we feel afraid, we are sure to experience physical and emotional pain as a result. We feel the physical, visceral sensation of fear. We experience the emotional torment of fear. Our perceptions and judgments become clouded. The energy patterns that arise because of the experience of fear can remain in our bodies for hours, days, weeks, or, for some individuals, an entire lifetime. Also, when we operate based on the charge of an emotion such as fear, we often make impulsive decisions that lead to more turmoil, drama, or difficulty. We may say things that in hindsight we know we shouldn't have said. We do things that we know are going to bite us in the back later, but we do them because our sense of caution has been overridden by adrenaline and stress.

Because of our strong attachment to the self, we are all obsessed with survival. We try to hold on to youth by eating healthy food and staying active. We remove our wrinkles and dye our hair. We face the dilemma of medical treatments that often cause more pain than our original illness, all in the name of survival. But the great masters of the Buddhist tradition were not worried about mere survival. They were most concerned with the *quality* of survival, both for themselves and others. They wanted to bring peace, health, well-being, and happiness to themselves and others. Because of the lofty nature of this goal, the way they thought, spoke, acted, and practiced spirituality was different than ordinary people in the world. They realized that the impulse to self-protect gives rise to painful emotions such as fear, anger, jealousy, attachment, pride, and greed. They realized that relaxing self-cherishing and conducting themselves differently than ordinary people brought them a happier state of mind.

Self-Love and Self-Protection

The great Buddhist masters have shown us that the greatest kind of self-love is to let go of the instinct to protect the self. Because all our reactions, feelings, and imbalances are amplified when we are trying to protect the self, it follows that the best way to bring a sense of spaciousness, relaxation, and comfort to ourselves and others is by relaxing the fear that others or outside situations will harm us. The advice of the great Buddhist masters is to drop our tendency to worry about things that are out of our control. *If there is something I can change, I should change it. There is no need to worry. If there is something I can't change, I should accept that it can't change. There is no need to worry.* Worrying doesn't protect us. It does not stop unwanted things from happening. Worrying does not help us handle things better, ensure our survival, or help us manipulate people and situations around us. Most simply put, worrying is an expression of self-cherishing that is the opposite of self-love. It undermines healthy habits such as feeling self-confident and capable. It keeps us from relaxing and feeling peace of mind.

Lojong masters such as Patrul Rinpoche took this advice even further. Not only did he drop the habit of self-protection, but he actively used the Buddhist teachings to reverse this tendency by putting himself in uncomfortable situations. He conveys this advice in his *Words of My Perfect Teacher*, saying, "When among others, always take the lower seat." These words convey a sense of placing others before us, both literally and through our words and actions. They express the idea that the person who cares less about where he or she sits is happier. The person who can fit in anywhere is the most comfortable everywhere. In this book, Patrul Rinpoche also recounts many stories about how the Kadampa masters of old lived by this same advice. One story recounts how the Kadampa master called Geshe Ben was sharing a meal with a large gathering of geshes at a place called Penyul-gyal in Tibet. He was sitting in the middle of the group, and there were many in the front rows being served yogurt before him. He wondered to himself if there would be any yogurt left by the time the servers got to him. Because of having this selfish wish to get something for himself, when it came his time to be served, Geshe Ben flipped his bowl over and didn't take any yogurt for himself. This was not an act of self-negation or self-punishment but rather the recognition that the wish to be treated as special would ultimately only lead to further suffering.

Patrul Rinpoche's advice applies to us in our time; it was not simply followed by the masters of old. Our own master, Tsara Dharmakirti Rinpoche, also lived by this advice. He took the *Way of a Bodhisattva* as one of his heart practices, taking this text with him everywhere he traveled. There are many stories of him living by the words of Patrul Rinpoche and the other lojong masters. One story recounts how, after the Communist restructuring of Tibet, he was placed in charge of the tent where food for the local village was collected and distributed. At that time, the villagers could only eat their quota of food, and the distribution of food was highly regulated. Because our master was respected and revered by others, the women who oversaw the milk collection offered in secret to let him have as much milk as he wanted. Tsara Dharmakirti Rinpoche loved milk, and one day he went into the tent and lifted the lid on a large vat of milk, thinking of scooping up a ladleful. But before he did so, he thought about the suffering caused by focusing on personal wishes and desires.

He put the lid back on the vat of milk and resolved to drink only black tea from then on.

These examples show that giving ourselves what we want isn't the only or the most effective way to feel happy or to love ourselves. Giving ourselves what we want is an expression of self-cherishing. Self-cherishing reinforces all the patterns that cause us suffering. It is worth taking some time to reflect on these ideas, and to experiment with what it would be like to apply them—even in small or seemingly insignificant ways.

We could try very simple ways of reversing this tendency. For example, the next time we are serving food, we can be sure to give others the better or more beautiful portions or we can let others go before us, even when we are in a great hurry. When we are driving, we can reverse the impulse to perceive other drivers as mere irritants and impediments to getting where we want to go by consciously extending courtesy and creating space for others. Imagine if everyone the world over were to begin acting in this way, how profoundly we could change our daily experience.

The Result of Grasping at the Body as Me

How can we understand the suffering that ensues from *not taking the lower seat*? Or the suffering that comes from following the impulse to self-protect and manipulate people and the world to make us feel comfortable? We can consider the answer to these questions from a physical as well as an emotional point of view.

First, when we follow the urge to self-protect, we identify intensely with the body, and so our physical and sensory experience is heightened and intense. We may or may not be aware of our initial reaction, but it will cause us pain sooner or later. Take the example of a mosquito bite. When a mosquito bites us, we may not even feel a sting. We may begin to scratch at it mindlessly, even before we have the presence of mind to realize that scratching it will make it itch or burn even more intensely. But how many of us have scratched at a mosquito bite, even though we realize it is going to make the bite itch more? If we identify with the physical experience of the mosquito bite too much—in other words, if we identify too much with the body's physical experience—we aren't going to be able to tolerate the bite without scratching. Sometimes we scratch it so much that the itching turns into pain. The bite begins to bleed and scab over, or it even becomes infected. All of this we may do even though we know the consequences, simply because our habit is to scratch what itches.

Thinking about a physical irritation as small as a mosquito bite can really illustrate how suffering arises based on attachment to the body. When our identification and attachment are untempered and intense, we cannot help ourselves—we automatically engage in behavior that irritates and agitates what is already painful. We hurt ourselves, even though we are doing our best to relieve our own suffering. Isn't this what we are doing all the time? When we attach to the physical experience of suffering, whether it be something as small as a mosquito bite or as painful as an illness such as cancer, even more pain is sure to follow.

Who Are We, Anyway?

Often when we think about realized spiritual masters, we become fearful instead of inspired. We may wonder what will happen to us if we stop protecting ourselves, or if we identify less with our bodies and emotions. We may question if we will even be able to relate to others anymore, or if we will just lose touch with normal people and the world. Will we be able to have a job, a spouse, a family? What will happen to us if we change the rules of the game of life?

Again, we can come back to the example of the lojong masters. Spiritual masters are highly relatable and highly functional people. They can fit in with all kinds of people, feel comfortable anywhere, and find creative solutions to problems that other people can't see. In short, spiritual development brings us closer to others rather than further away from them. When we drop the urge to protect ourselves, we can relate more directly with others. We stop disconnecting, avoiding, and running away. We are free to develop ways to deal with the same habits and problems that have been troubling us all along.

The Dalai Lama is a wonderful example of how a spiritual master lives in the modern world, bringing harmony and well-being to those around him. He is highly skillful at talking with others and exhibits great flexibility and adaptability in his personal connections. There are probably very few people, if any, who think of the Dalai Lama as a being who has lost his ability to connect with others or deal with the trials and hardships of life.

Notice the Impulse to Self-Protect as Lojong

The impulse to self-protect is with us all the time. We can begin to notice this impulse in all of its strengths and variations. Even if we cannot drop this impulse in the moment, we can at least remember that we have a choice as to how we deal with things.

In the *Way of a Bodhisattva*, Shantideva teaches that the criticism of others cannot really harm us. It may be extremely painful to bear, and there are times when it can cause us to feel literally attacked. It may cause strong reactions in us such as stress or fear, but the words, gestures, and body language of others do not threaten our survival. Many other situations in life that also seem to threaten our very being, such as the loss of something we think we need—a job, the support of a close relationship, or a living situation that makes us feel safe and comfortable—may cause us stress or fear. But rather than giving in to our normal emotional patterns when these difficult situations come up, we could choose to practice lojong.

In these kinds of situations, we can mentally reflect on whether our emotional response is appropriate in light of what happened. Often the intensity of our emotions is not really warranted by the situation. However, if we decide that the situation does justify a strong response, we can also reflect on whether or not our response benefits ourselves, others, and our overall spiritual development. Is the end result happiness, peace of mind, and well-being? Do worry and anxiety help to change what has happened? Or would it be more beneficial to reflect on the life examples of Geshe Ben, Patrul Rinpoche, and Tsara Dharmakirti Rinpoche, who realized that being special and getting what we want are not the true causes of happiness?

Even in the case of something that does threaten our survival, such as an illness or being in a car accident, we can still choose how much power to give this experience. We do not have to avoid the experience or attempt to forget it. Nor do we need to focus on it or put too much attention upon it. When we feel worry, fear, or anxiety, we can call to mind the words of the Buddhist masters, who said, "If what happened cannot be changed, why worry? If it can be changed, why worry?" We can recognize that acceptance of whatever is happening right now brings us the greatest peace and clarity of mind.

Great spiritual masters such as our master Tsara Dharmakirti Rinpoche were able to face even threats of mortal harm fearlessly and without stress or strong emotional reactions. Sometime after the revolution in Tibet, Tsara Dharmakirti Rinpoche was riding a beautiful white horse through the eastern part of the country. He left a monastery in Amdo Trokyab and rode to the part of Tibet called Tsorung. One morning while he was sleeping, soldiers came to his camp and started shooting at him. Tsara Dharmakirti Rinpoche was in his thirties at that time. He took hold of his horse and saddled it, then jumped on and rode away. Startled by the gunfire, his horse grew wild and bucked him off. Our lama broke his humerus, the bone in his upper right arm, when he fell. The break never healed, and for the rest of his life his arm just dangled, held together by only skin and flesh. On that day he had been wearing the very thick sheepskin clothing Tibetans call *gak*. That night, when he unwrapped the gak, many bullets fell to the ground, as they had struck but not penetrated his body. Although the heavy clothing protected him from bullet wounds, he had deep bruises from where he was struck.

Later, when asked if these experiences had caused him pain, our lama only smiled. He continued to use his broken arm to do prostrations every day throughout his life. The bone jutted out of the skin as he used that broken arm to move up and down. He was never known to complain of pain or discomfort even once during his life.

As we start to notice our own responses and how often we feel personally attacked by people and the situations we encounter in our lives, we can treat this noticing as a mindfulness practice, slowly teaching ourselves to become more and more aware of how sensitive we are and how strong our feelings of self-protectiveness are. We can also reflect on how the development of spiritual qualities such as openness, love, and compassion is obstructed by our self-protective feelings, which cause us to disconnect from others or fight with them. When we begin to relax this impulse to self-protect, we start to accept situations as they are. From there we can uncover a broader range of skillful ways to respond.

5

Applying Lojong to the Five Aggregates

IN CHAPTERS 3 and 4, we reflected on the deep attachment and self-cherishing that we have toward our physical bodies and emotional experiences. As we discussed, this seemingly natural self-cherishing directs everything we do. It is the instigator of our energy patterns, reactions, words, body language and gestures, and actions. Although we may have had our own ideas about who our friends and enemies were in the past, once we recognize how intense our self-cherishing is, we can begin to know it as our true enemy. All the other enemies we may have perceived in our lifetimes are nothing in comparison to self-cherishing. They have neither its strength nor its tenacity. From the point of view of karma, the suffering they have caused us is merely incidental, as they have simply stepped into our lives and become entangled in the self-cherishing that is our preexisting condition. Even for those who have experienced severe suffering at the hands of another person, the only way to undo the effects of this is to address the enemy of our emotional patterns and habits within.

There are some things we are powerless to change. We can't always change the circumstances we find ourselves in, and we can't change events that have happened in the past, no matter how happy, sad, beautiful, or tragic they may have been. But we can always work on how we react to them and how much we allow them to influence our energy, hearts, and minds here and now.

How painful this life we live, each of us entangling the other in our own ambitious plans for happiness, each of us failing to be content with what we have, unable to enjoy the good things that come to us.

Until now, we may have told many stories to ourselves and others to explain or justify what has happened to us in our lives. We may have thought long and hard about how others caused us to suffer needlessly or unjustly. But if we take the time to look in the mirror, we begin to see through the storylines of our personal drama. We realize that our self-cherishing is the author, the director, and the star of everything that is happening around us. These outer enemies are just our partners in the dance of life, here for a moment and then gone. But our thoughts, feelings, and reactions to the people and events in our lives have endured, making these momentary encounters ever present and vivid within the mind. Thus our attachment to momentary happiness and suffering stays with us, and we have roiled in misery as a result.

A true bodhisattva, a real spiritual hero, is brave enough to look in the mirror. A true hero is brave enough to recognize that the enemy we all face is dwelling within.

This dance of life is not inherently good or bad. It is always changing. If we are mindless, we whirl around from here to there, too dizzy to take deliberate action and find a definite course. When luck is with us we may dance beautifully. When luck is against us, we may stumble and fall. With great effort, we may catch our balance and continue the dance without missing a step. Ultimately it is up to us. One thing we can be sure of, though. If we can keep looking in the mirror, and keep the focus on our own minds, motivations, and actions, we are sure to become more skillful at the dance of life, becoming people who can bring peace of mind to both ourselves and others.

The spiritual path can be our source of optimism. If we are willing to walk the path of these great lojong masters, we are bound to find some of the peace of mind they found. Sooner or later we can defeat this great enemy of self-cherishing that dwells within.

After reflecting long and hard on our own self-cherishing, we might wonder what other tools Buddhism has for decreasing our self-attachment. After all, if we were great heroes going into battle with powerful foes, we would be sure that we had a variety of weapons and resources available to us. The great lojong master Gyalsé Togmé Zangpo refers to the inner weapons we need as spiritual armor, which can help us ensure that we won't be pierced by the swords and spears of our self-cherishing and our strong emotions. How do we find this kind of spiritual armor? If we are following the teachings of the bodhisattva path, all the protection that we need is right at our fingertips.

Remember that developing the quality of patience is like putting on bulletproof armor that can keep us safe in any situation. Patience can heal any wound, calm any disturbance, and dissolve any pain. Patience helps us see what options are before us, what the consequences of our actions are. It is ultimately like our eyes that can see the road ahead. Even though we may be walking on a path covered with thorns, patience is like a thick-soled pair of shoes that makes our journey possible. Especially when we are taking up the bodhisattva path, we will need to sip the elixir of patience as often as we can. Remember, the habit of self-cherishing is so strong that we cannot gain much ground against it. And what ground we do gain is easily lost. Lojong is not something that we can master in a few hours, days, weeks, or even years. The path of lojong takes repeated effort throughout our lives.

Our lama, Tsara Dharmakirti Rinpoche, describes it this way: When we work to change ourselves, we are like a crooked stick that has become wet and malleable. While the stick is still wet, it can be straightened and made to stay that way. But the minute the stick dries, it goes right back to its original shape. If we wish to maintain our practice over a long time, we practitioners of lojong should always keep these wise words in mind. When we try to change our own shape, we will find that we are successful for a time. But when we face a stressful or difficult situation that pushes our buttons, we will go right back to how we used to be. It is extremely painful to regress back to old habits and to see ourselves acting just as we used to. But this is all part of the process of training the mind. When we take another good look in the mirror and are properly sobered with the knowledge of who we are—as opposed to who we think we are or who we pretend to be—we can start again and refocus our efforts on reducing our self-cherishing and putting others first.

Working with the Five Aggregates

The attachment to the physical body and emotional experience explored previously can be examined in the context of what are called *the five aggregates*. Thinking about the self as composed of "aggregates" (Skt. *skandha*) can help us reflect on our personal identity in new ways. Generally, we attribute characteristics to our personal identity, feeling that it is solid, permanent, and real. But here, describing the self as being composed of aggregates can help us see ourselves more accurately. The word *skandha* can be translated literally as "heap." This definition, when applied to ourselves, can help us see that we do not have a cohesive, real, and solid self. We are just a heap of stuff—flesh, blood, veins, nerves, bones, hair, cartilage, and so on. When we sort through this heap, what are we actually? None of the elements of the heap is actually "me." We are a mere mishmash of material conditions that we have identified with and labeled "I."

In this same way, everything and everyone we encounter are just heaps of stuff—what we call *causes and conditions*—one piled on top of another. For example, an apple is a heap of material conditions such as skin, flesh, sugar, moisture, and seeds.

That apple is also composed of causes that are the basis of it appearing in just this way—the coming together of soil, water, nutrients, light, warmth, and a seed in just the right way. The difference is that when we see an apple we label it, calling it an apple. We identify with it—my apple, the kind of apple I like, the kind of apple I don't like, an apple I need to buy to possess it, an apple I can eat right now because I own it. We see that apple through the lens of "me." We don't see that apple as a heap of causes and conditions—a mere form.

Saying that something is a heap or formed by aggregates is another way of saying that it is *dependently arisen*, or that it is arisen from causes and conditions. It is not truly existent in the way that our minds ordinarily see us, others, and the world around us. For this reason we say that the individual self and all phenomena are not truly existent. These five aggregates are the building blocks of all our experience.

First, the Aggregate of Form

The first aggregate is called the *aggregate of form*. This aggregate is the basis for the way that we relate to the phenomenal world and ourselves, since the body is the cause of self-attachment. The Buddha Shakyamuni defines *form* as being the heap of causes and conditions that have color and shape, or any tangible quality to them. Form is our strongest attachment. The great Buddhist scholar Chandrakirti says that after first thinking "I," we grasp at the self, and then based on that self-grasping, we superimpose and grasp at everything else we come in contact with as "mine." Thus our entire conceptual framework is based on the relationship between I and mine—my body, my self, my feelings, my perceptions, my choices, my experiences, my spouse, my family, my job, my house, and so on.

This tenuous relationship between I and mine can be broken down as we contemplate the transient quality of form. For example, we can reflect in this way: Understand the heap of causes and conditions that create any form—the physical body, for example—to be like a bubble. When we see a bubble on the surface of water, we have no idea when it will break. It is so fragile. As soon as we see it, we are already aware that it won't last long. We know it could pop at any moment.

When we perceive form, our innate habit is to think it is lasting and permanent. But no form is like that. No matter what form it is, whether it be square, flat, or round, no matter what color it is, it makes no difference. It is just a heap of conditions that happen to have a tangible quality. Because it is not solid, real, and lasting, it could disappear at any moment, just like a bubble popping. It could change its appearance completely. When we reflect in this manner, we can begin to unravel the attachment that we have toward form—even our own form.

We can also apply lojong to notice how different afflictive emotions arise because of our attachment to form. When we see a form that we find beautiful or pleasing, we immediately generate attachment to it. When we see something ugly or repulsive, we feel dislike, unhappiness, or sometimes even anger because we don't like what we see. When we see something that we feel neutral toward or don't care about, we generate neutrality or indifference. All these different emotions are reactions to the sense of sight.

Apply Lojong Using the Heart Sutra

When we recite a text such as the *Heart Sutra*, we can use the words of the text to contemplate the dependently arisen nature of phenomena and break down the attachment we have toward the forms we perceive in the world around us. The method of reflecting on the *Heart Sutra* that follows may be different than what we have heard before. It follows the contemplative tradition of Ju Mipham Rinpoche and other great scholars of the Nyingma tradition of Tibetan Buddhism, who focus on *the empty quality of apparent phenomena*. This is a philosophical way of saying that all things that appear—that is, apparent phenomena—and that can be perceived by any of our five senses are empty. That is, they have no lasting or real essence. Although forms that appear can be perceived, they're not "real" in the way we think they are. A short text such as the *Heart Sutra* is the perfect vehicle for cultivating this understanding.

First, let's take a moment to make sure we understand the meaning of some of the lines of the *Heart Sutra*. (The whole text of the *Heart Sutra* can be found in the appendix on pages 141–44.) We can first reflect on the idea that "form is empty, emptiness is form." The first thing to understand from these words is that anything dependently arisen—in other words, a heap of causes and conditions such as a person or an apple—must be *empty*. What is it empty of? It is empty of any real, lasting, or solid self-identity, just as we have been discussing above. To contemplate this line reminds us of the depth of our confusion about the nature of form. We innately believe that forms are real, solid, and lasting. But, actually, they are empty. A form is just a heap of stuff piled together, which has appeared as a form that we have perceived, which we have then named, and to which we have attributed an identity.

We are attached to all different kinds of form. We are attached to our own form and that of other beings; we are attached to color, shape, beauty, and our perception of what is good, bad, or neutral. Whenever we are looking at something—for example, a particular color or shape—if we can reflect on it as being a heap of stuff, saying "form is empty, emptiness is form," then eventually the knowledge of that as an impermanent appearance will dawn within the mind. The attachment, the tendency to see things as lasting or permanent, will be reduced.

We can reflect on an extreme example to see why this kind of lojong practice will benefit us. It is easy to look at a book, a vase of flowers, or a beautiful spring day and say "form is empty, emptiness is form." But say our spouse is angry with us and yells at us for something that in reality we didn't do. In that moment, when he or she is shouting at us unjustly, do we remember that "form is empty, emptiness is form"? Probably not. Instead, we immediately react to it. We're completely overpowered by the appearance of the situation at hand. We identify with it. It feels real. It looks real.

If we cannot recognize the emptiness of forms and appearances in ordinary, neutral situations, how will we ever do so when the situation is emotionally charged? We are constantly overpowered by thinking that appearances are real and that the world around us is real. To change this habit, we will have to become adept at reflecting on the impermanent nature of forms. This reflection will help us gain certainty that this is true. Without it, our identification with ourselves and the phenomenal world is so strong that it can overpower us. It can make it seem that our contemplative ideas lack merit, and that the only thing that is real is this situation in front of us, which we need to protect ourselves from. When we begin to realize that forms are just impermanent heaps of stuff, with no real, solid, or lasting identities, our emotional responses lessen. When this happens, our spouse yelling at us for something we didn't do doesn't seem like such a big deal. This does not just become some subtle way of shutting out our spouse. Because we are less attached to ourselves, there is less at stake and less need to protect ourselves. We can be more open to feedback, more open to what is happening around us or with another person, because we are not driven merely by the impulse to protect ourselves.

The most important form that we could contemplate using the *Heart Sutra* is our own physical body—this form that we believe is "me." After all, if we wish to curb the intensity of our emotional responses and bring feelings of peace to our minds, we can achieve this only by reducing our self-cherishing. When we begin to release some of that attachment we have to the self, we have fewer emotional outbursts. When the mind begins to relax, we have less anger, less attachment, and less ignorance. We also grasp less toward the things outside of us. If we grasp at ourselves less, then we also don't identify so much with the things around us, thinking, *That's mine and I need to protect it*, or *I need to have this*, or *I need it to be this way*. When we relax our self-cherishing, everything that feels complicated about life begins to slowly relax. No matter what is happening in any moment or what has happened in the past, we may not feel great but we can feel basically okay. We can feel less sensitive and less injured by life.

Contemplate the Remaining Senses

In addition to the sense of sight, which perceives the appearance of form, we also grasp at our other sensory experiences: sound, smell, taste, and touch. These are also part of the aggregate of form. The *Heart Sutra* mentions each of these as well. In addition to saying that form is empty, it also says that there are "no sounds, no smells, no tastes, no tactile sensations." This is not to suggest that we do not experience each of the five senses on a relative level. Rather, what it means is that just like forms that appear, each of our other sensory experiences is also dependently arisen and therefore empty.

We can take the example of the sound of someone's voice. How is sound empty? Being able to perceive the sound of someone's voice is based on many causes and conditions coming together: the presence of the person articulating the voice, the physical expression of the voice, the exhalation of the breath as the person speaks, the inhalation of the breath, and the perceiver of the sound. We cannot say that the sound is any one of these things; it is the expression of them all coming together. It is empty.

Even though sound is empty, we still react to it with a multitude of emotions. For example, we may love the sound of a songbird and cringe when we hear a car alarm. We might have a strong reaction to the words or the message conveyed by a voice rather than the voice itself. Depending on the specific circumstances, attachment or anger comes up right on the spot. We can begin to notice how there is no space between sensory perception and our emotional response—they seem to arise simultaneously.

By relying on the *Heart Sutra*, we can begin to put space in between our perceptions and our reactions. When we hear a sound we could think, *Sound is nothing other than emptiness; emptiness resounds as sound.* Using the analytical quality of the mind, we can turn our attention away from its tendency to react to the sound and let the sound fade away on its own.

In the same way described above, all sensory experiences are also dependently arisen and are empty of any true and lasting nature. We can take time to reflect on the dependently arisen nature of smell, taste, and touch, using the *Heart Sutra* to poke holes in their seemingly solid natures.

Another Way to Apply Lojong to Sensory Experience

Sensory experience itself is not inherently negative. It does not have to be the cause of strong afflictive emotions. When we practice meditation, we are not trying to shut down the mind or the sensory experience. We are trying to relax the mind and its painful habit of self-cherishing, not to disengage from the world. Take the example of perfectly mindful and realized lojong masters such as Atisha, Shantideva, and Patrul Rinpoche. These masters allow sensory experiences to arise within themselves and then dissolve, without generating any emotional reactions or attachments whatsoever. For them, sensory experience is a source of energy that enables them to connect with and understand others, that guides them in a manner that benefits others, and that teaches them how to interact skillfully with others and the environment.

In order to change our habitual responses and reactions, we must first get to know ourselves a bit better. Take some time to explore your attachment to sensory experience. There are several methods you could use to begin to get a sense of the dense attachment you have to your inner world. Try examining each one of your senses and sensory experiences, in turn, in a contemplative manner. First, reflect on and examine the attachment you have toward form. *How do I feel when I see something beautiful? How do I react to something that appears horrifying or disgusting? What about when I see something that I feel indifferent to?*

In each case, it is likely that your attachment toward what you see is instantaneous and visceral. The Buddhist teachings describe perception as being such a deep and subtle habit that it can be thought of as intrinsic or innate. You can start to notice what kind of reaction it causes in both the body and mind. Sometimes, if your reaction is extremely strong, you will notice a disturbance in your body and mind that can last for several hours or even a whole day. This speaks to how strong your attachment and reaction are to that sensory experience. Even when the experience has passed, it often lingers as though it is ongoing and present.

Next, contemplate each of the other senses in exactly the same way. *How do I react to smell, taste, sound, and touch?* Start your contemplation using sensory objects that you find enticing and seductive. Then continue contemplating by reflecting on experiences you dislike or that make you feel uncomfortable. Finally, what is your reaction to sensory objects that neither draw nor repel you, to which you are indifferent?

It is likely that just reflecting on sensory attachment as a mental exercise isn't enough to help you notice the strength and quality of your reactivity toward sensory experience. It is difficult to recognize just how sensitive each of us is. In this case, we can examine our sensitivity using more potent methods.

Work at a Deeper Level

To get a more direct sense of the intensity of your attachment to sensory experience, purposefully put yourself in situations where you will have strong and noticeable reactions. This is a very traditional style of Buddhist examination and contemplation. For example, you may want to visit a museum, a carnival, a flower shop, an expensive store, or any other place where you might encounter something beautiful. Then visit a place where you are sure to encounter something distasteful—the back alleyway where trash is kept, a room full of bright lights, or a shop full of clothing you dislike. You can also use photographs, movies, or any daily activities that are suitable. You want to be sure to look at a variety of objects, so that you notice the whole range of reactions you have toward things that you see. *How do I feel when I see something I want? Something I love? Something I don't want? Something I hate? What kind of change happens in my body, my mind, my thoughts? What sensations are present within my body when those changes come?*

You can do the same for each of the other senses. When examining your reactions to smell, be sure to smell something fragrant or delicious and something distasteful, as well as something neutral. When examining your reactions to sound, listen to a range of sounds. Listen to an intense, piercing sound such as a car alarm, or turn on the television loudly while you try to practice or have a quiet conversation. Listen to a song that brings back a sad memory. Fill the room with white noise. Taste a range of flavors—sweet, salty, bitter. Then taste water, which has no special flavor at all. To explore touch, touch different fabrics or surfaces that are silky, smooth, rough, or sharp. In all these cases, notice the range of reactions you have. Notice how certain sensory experiences trigger emotions, thought patterns, or tie up your energy in other ways. *Just how sensitive am I? How does what I experience affect my state of mind?*

And Even Deeper

You may also want to try this exercise in an even more engaged manner. You can start by choosing one of your five senses to be the subject of your examination when you wake up in the morning. Start with sight. During the day, try to notice the range of reactions you have toward the things you see. You can continue this engaged exploration of sensory attachment by choosing a different sense to focus on for each day that follows. Use your daily life as the grounds for your personal research.

• • •

As we probably discovered when engaging in the exercises presented earlier in this chapter, many of the sights and sounds we encounter during the day can cause strong emotional reactions within us. One example is the visceral reaction we may have to the sound of someone's voice when he or she says something we don't want to hear in a tone we don't like. In a moment like that, how do we practice lojong to relieve our sensitivity toward sound?

As soon as we notice that we are having a strong reaction to the sound of someone's voice, we can try to kindle patience. We can work with any contemplative tool that helps to reduce our reaction. We can reflect on how the sound of his or her voice is such a small cause for such a strong emotional reaction. We can also reflect on what feelings the other person may be having, or what situation he or she may be facing, that caused him or her to say something we didn't want to hear. This can help us realize that the person is also facing personal difficulties. Finally, we might also notice the strong sense of self-attachment that we have, how easily we are injured by the mere words of another or the sound of his or her voice. Rather than blaming the other person, we could renew our commitment to place others first and focus less on ourselves. Applying the bodhisattva path is an extremely effective method for cutting through the intense attachment we have to the five senses and the aggregate of form.

Second, the Aggregate of Feeling

Even though we began our reflection on the five aggregates with form, we cannot stop our investigation there, because form isn't the only thing we identify with. In addition to form, there are four additional aggregates that also contribute to our sense of self: feeling, perception, karmic formation, and consciousness.

The *aggregate of feeling* brings us inconceivable suffering. As we discussed in chapter 3, the attachment to our feelings is completely overwhelming. We don't generally have the sense that our emotions are impermanent at all. We see our emotions as being unchanging, real, and sometimes all-powerful. Not only that, but we are also raised in a culture where we are taught that our feelings are important. We are taught to hold on to our feelings, to act upon our feelings, to express them, to resolve them, and to respond to them. The way that we relate to our feelings has shaped our whole culture. In Western culture, as opposed to the culture of an Asian country such as Tibet, feelings and self-cherishing have really become one and the same thing. Whenever we are attached to, or responding to, our feelings, we are expressing self-attachment. Feelings and self-attachment are just like fire and warmth; one has the qualities of the other. We can also think of feelings as being like the water that turns the waterwheel of our self-attachment. It serves as its energy and provides its momentum.

Just as the *Heart Sutra* states that "form is empty, emptiness is form," it also says that none of the other four aggregates truly exist. Just as form is empty and has no real or lasting essence, there is no feeling, perception, karmic formation, or consciousness. We can come back to these words as we attempt to stay balanced by putting less weight on our feelings, or any of the other aggregates as well.

Third, the Aggregate of Perception

We also identify intensely with the aspect of self called *perception*. What do the teachings say about the *aggregate of perception*? It describes perception as being like a water mirage.

We have probably all had an experience like this. We are driving down the highway in the middle of summer. It is burning hot outside; heat seeps out of the asphalt. There is a pool of water on the highway in front of us, and we drive toward the water expecting to reach it. But the closer that we get to the pool of water, the farther away it moves. This illustration describes how our perception, which we believe to be true and real, is also empty and dependently arisen. This is not to say that we haven't "seen" the water mirage. But our perception is inaccurate because we attributed qualities of materiality to something that was never actually there.

The biggest misperception we all share is that we will find true and lasting happiness based on ordinary, worldly life. We perceive that treating loved ones as friends and those we dislike as enemies will ensure that we are safe, protected, and happy. We perceive that it is possible to achieve happiness by controlling people and events so that we can make things just so. As a result, we may spend our whole lives chasing after the lives that we think we deserve. But in the end, our efforts will be fruitless. Just like a mule deer chasing after a water mirage who ultimately dies of thirst, we will be destined to remain unsatisfied. Why is this so?

From the outset, we were never going to get what we wanted. We may have had a perception that things were going to turn out a certain way, but just like that water mirage, most things that we hope for and expect never materialize. Still, when we think we see the illusory thing, we attach to it right on the spot, even though it isn't really there.

How does our perception contribute to our strong emotional patterns? First, when we trust our perceptions completely, we think, *My way is the right way.* This confusion causes conflict with other people because it strengthens our self-cherishing. Our perception of events may also cause us to think that what other people said or did is wrong. We might think, *Their way is wrong.* Again, this creates conflict. The self-attachment that causes the thought "My way is right and your way is wrong" will result sooner or later in the sufferings of judgment, self-righteousness, criticism, anger, or any number of other emotional responses. We will suffer just like the thirsty mule deer.

Our perceptions are also colored by our feelings and beliefs to the extent that none of us can see clearly. For example, we may enter a room and see a friend who doesn't greet us as warmly as we expect. Although our friend may be distracted, struggling with strong emotions or a difficult situation that is wholly unrelated to us, we may perceive he or she dislikes us. Once we have begun to perceive things in this manner, we may also fall into the habit of gathering evidence to support our belief. We may watch our friend more closely, trying to notice if our friend's gestures, body language, or tone of voice show us that he or she dislikes us. In the interest of our self-cherishing and our instinct to self-protect, we may be strengthening a conflict that never existed in the first place.

A final example is how a strong emotion such as fear clouds our perceptions. We may have a strong fear that a certain place is dangerous. That feeling of fear causes us to perceive actual danger even if the place is safe. We can see this to be true even from the example of a child entering into a supposedly haunted house. Although there is nothing truly frightening present, the child's fear makes it frightening.

Fourth, the Aggregate of Karmic Formation

The fourth aggregate, described here as *karmic formation*, is referred to by a number of different names depending on the text or translator. In this case, we can use the name "karmic formation" to help us understand the character of this aggregate more thoroughly. One way to understand the word *formation* is as a reference to our belief that we are building lives for ourselves. In doing so, we are accumulating the things that we want and trying to get rid of the things that we don't. These things we are accumulating are in the process of becoming, or forming. The word *karmic* refers to the way that formation occurs. All the conditions in our lives are manifesting due to the motivations and actions that we have had in the past and that we have now. So our lives are not randomly developing. Formation occurs in accordance with our own habits and tendencies.

How do the teachings describe karmic formation? The traditional metaphor used to describe karmic formation is a rotten log. On the outside, the log looks solid and healthy. But we know that if the log is rotten, sooner or later it is going to fall apart. These lives that we are living, the people we love, the people we hate, the things we have, the things we don't have—all of this is building and accumulating, but has no real and lasting essence. Sooner or later it will all be lost. It will all fall apart. In the end, we won't have gained anything.

When we contemplate karmic formation, we can reflect on how everything that comes together is going to fall apart. This is the basis of karma, the law of cause and effect. Things come together; they separate. Causes and conditions manifest, and things change. Our lives are like rotten logs. We think of them as being solid and sure, not realizing that they could fall apart at any moment.

The metaphor of the rotten log points out that the way we relate to ourselves and our emotions is fundamentally mistaken. We are focusing on building the wrong things. If everything in our ordinary lives is going to fall apart, shouldn't we put more energy into our spiritual practice? Shouldn't we focus on something that can bring us peace of mind? After all, our lives are fleeting; they won't last forever. Sooner or later we will be facing the swift-flowing rivers of old age, sickness, and death. Although our loved ones may wish to help us at that time when those rivers begin to overwhelm us, spiritual practice is the only friend that will keep us company as we face the moment of death. It is the only thing we can truly depend on.

The aggregate of karmic formation can remind us that where we put our energy now will ripen as the positive or negative conditions we will face in the future. If we continue putting our energy into the same emotional habits and patterns that have been troubling us all along, we are sure to experience the same results that have been manifesting all along.

When we rely upon the proper foundation, spiritual practice can be the catalyst to change our karma and habitual patterns for the better. When we generate the mind of bodhichitta, wishing to place all sentient beings, including ourselves, in the state beyond suffering, we cut through the self-cherishing that pervades every aspect of our lives. The result is that we can put an end to the self-fulfilling prophecy of suffering.

Fifth, the Aggregate of Consciousness

The Buddhist teachings describe the final aggregate, the *aggregate of consciousness*, as being like an illusion. This metaphor refers to the mind itself. We think the mind is real. We think the mind is the essence of "me." But the mind is impermanent. The mind has no shape, form, color, or location. Nobody can pin-point exactly what it is. For example, is it the heart? The brain? The impulses of the nervous system? Our thought patterns? Our deep beliefs and values? The complexity and mystery of the mind make it fairly easy to see that the mind itself is ephemeral and fleeting, with no lasting or permanent essence. When we con-template whether there is any real or lasting self, we can add to it our understanding that the mind is certainly too vast and com-plex to be pigeonholed as "me."

Although we put tremendous energy into believing our minds, our thoughts, and our emotions are real, lasting, and permanent, they're just like bubbles arising on top of this fleeting concept of "me." We can't actually keep a single state of mind for long, even if we try. Even though this is the case, we identify with our minds, our thoughts, and our ideas at each and every moment.

It is quite freeing to drop this kind of self-identification. Many times, our thoughts, ideas, and even the mind itself have an in-tense energetic charge that is difficult to harness and control. We may even fear all the energy arising in the mind and arising as thoughts. But because our thoughts are fleeting, insubstantial, and impermanent, they have no ability to hurt us, no matter how powerful they seem. They are just like vapor, which appears and disappears without a trace.

Finally, Take Stock

What do we conclude from this exploration of the five aggregates and the *Heart Sutra*? We have reflected on how everything that we see, hear, smell, taste, and touch appears but has no lasting es-sence. Even this "I" that we grasp at isn't really essentially "me." It is merely the five aggregates heaped together, which we have then identified with as the self. But this self we love and cherish so much isn't what we think it is—it appears just like a magical display before us and is changing at every moment.

With all of this in mind, we can take some time to reflect on the strength of our emotional reactions. *Do I really have so much to protect? Or is this feeling that I need to protect myself just another miscalculation? Is there another approach that might serve me better?* Contemplating how much pain and suffering stem from our emotional responses, we can take some time to question whether continuing the patterns we have fallen into in the past are really worth it. Are we truly benefited by grasping at and acting out strong emotions? Or could this be another mistake, just as we were wrong about who and what we are?

6

Finding a Friend in Lojong

LOJONG PRACTICE is crucial for any spiritual practitioner who wants to make a transformative change. As we have seen from the examples of the lineage masters who have come before us, when we begin to cut through feelings of self-cherishing and self-centeredness, we can experience the gift of relaxation in body and mind. Slowly, moment by moment, feelings of contentment and happiness dawn within us. When these happy moments arise, it is good to take note of them and value them as inspiration to persevere with the hard work of chiseling away at our self-cherishing.

But now that we have begun the hard work of noticing our negative habits and faults and attempting to lessen them, we may become overwhelmed by all the hard work yet to come. Imagine trying to destroy all our negative thought patterns at once. How much effort would that take? How painful would it be? Who would we be without this collection of thoughts and emotional patterns that we have now? We may experience moments of fear as our personal identities begin to soften and even slip away from us. But it is good to remember that our personal identities have never been the cause of peace, happiness, and well-being in the first place. On the contrary, they have been the very source of our suffering, as we have refused to accept the realities of life and continually chase after the lives we wish we had, like a pot of gold on the far side of the rainbow. Instead, when we notice that our sense of self is beginning to blur, we can feel incredibly encouraged. These feelings of fear can transform into a sense of rejoicing. After all, what could be better than softening who we are, shedding old layers, and becoming something fresh and new?

We can also take comfort in the fact that mind training is a gradual process. Although we are moving into new territory with this mind training, personal change doesn't happen quickly. We are fully capable of adjusting to who we are becoming if we don't succumb to anxiety or dive into a vat of fear. Mind training is a slow and natural process. As we begin to take on healthier behavior patterns, the old patterns that we don't need any longer begin to fall away naturally. We become less enamored of our negative habits, more aware of how they cause difficulties for ourselves and others. We are gradually more and more motivated to steer away from them. In the Buddhist teachings, we call this process *purification*. A buddha, or any realized master of the Buddhist tradition, is said to have manifested all good qualities and completely purified all negative habits. How exciting it is to be walking the same path as these great masters of wisdom! The cultivation of healthy behavior always goes hand in hand with the abandonment and purification of negative habits. As long as we keep working at training the mind, and at applying these teachings to gradually transform our thoughts and behaviors, we will notice that our negative patterns naturally fall away and a happier and healthier state of mind results. It is a perfectly organic process.

If we really stop and think about it, mind training is nothing new to us. But how have we been training our minds up until now? We should take an honest look. The majority of us have spent our lives training the mind in feelings of unhappiness and dissatisfaction. We have fed and reinforced these patterns with our feelings, attitudes, and actions. We have continually focused on what we don't have, what we wish was different, how others or the environment around us need to change so we can feel better. We have wasted enormous energy by trying to fortify ourselves, our belongings, and our loved ones from the inevitable forces of change. But even as we admit this to ourselves, there is no need to get into feelings of self-deprecation. This isn't our fault. Everyone and everything in our lives has taught us to be this way. We have always favored our friends and kept our enemies at arm's length. We have continually used our emotions to keep us safe, not realizing that it is those strong emotions that have made us unstable. Now we have the opportunity to take this basic habit of mind training and use it to transform ourselves and our seemingly fundamental patterns.

As we become more committed to the practice of mind training, there will be times when we realize we are different than who we thought we were. We may feel disappointed and embarrassed by who we have been in the past. Or we may struggle, sometimes unsuccessfully, to give up habits that we have been relying upon our whole lives. When we face these kinds of disappointments, it is essential not to fall into berating ourselves, but rather to encourage ourselves to keep going. After all, this is the natural and organic process of purification. Sooner or later, if we put in enough time and make enough effort, even the most deeply entrenched patterns will fall away. We need only trust ourselves, our practice, and the natural process of lojong.

Reflecting on What We Have

Feelings of dissatisfaction are often accompanied by a poverty mentality. Many of us feel we do not have what we need. We are afraid we do not have enough. And we are afraid to share the little we feel we do have with others. After all, what if we give someone else the very thing that we need for ourselves? What will happen then?

This attitude of mental poverty pervades our culture and our society, and it is worth questioning. *Am I truly impoverished, or is this just a fearful state of mind playing a trick on me?* According to the approach taken by the Buddhist teachings, this poverty mentality is just another expression of our self-cherishing. When our eyes are clouded by self-cherishing, and we are focused on all the things we think we need to be happy and healthy, it is easy to become stuck in the feeling that we don't have enough, that the things we have are inadequate. But with a simple change of attitude we can release ourselves from this feeling.

The Buddhist teachings help us open up this restrictive way of thinking by enabling us to recognize that each and every one of us has what is called *a precious human life*. This precious human life is the means for accomplishing the things we all want the most—to find happiness and relieve ourselves and others from suffering. The only thing we are required to do is train the mind in altruism. By turning our focus away from our selfish thoughts and toward the dharma, there is no reason to have a feeling of scarcity or poverty. The blessings that we receive when we take up the spiritual path cannot be taken away by anyone, but they can be bound up by self-attachment. We might even go so far as to say that blessings vanish as soon as self-cherishing shows its face.

Why is this human life so precious? The general Buddhist teachings give many explanations and metaphors that point out how rare and special it is to take birth as a human being as opposed to some other type of being living in this world. For example, if we compare the probability of taking birth as a human to the possibility of taking birth as an insect, or better yet, a microorganism, we can appreciate that it is quite marvelous that we are who we are. It is billions of times more likely that we would take birth as some other kind of organism or creature rather than as the people we are. The Buddhist teachings also point out how humans have many special qualities not shared by other animals or other beings on the planet, such as the ability to use and understand language; the ability to hear, understand, and apply spiritual teachings; and the ability to transform the mind. Perhaps as we continually delved into feelings of mental poverty and discontentment we did not spend much time reflecting on the lives we have as sources of richness and possibility. We may never have really thought about how much worse things could be, and thus may never have seen the goodness in our present circumstances.

As part of the Longchen Nyingthig lineage teachings, the omniscient Longchenpa gives a clear explanation that helps us see what it really means to value the life that we have. In this explanation, Longchenpa classifies the human life in three ways. The first is called having a *mere human life*, the second is called having an *adequate human life*, and the third is called having a *precious human life*.

The Mere Human Life

Longchenpa defines a *mere human life* as being lived by people whose motivation and conduct does not distinguish between right and wrong, and who put themselves and their own needs in the center of everything. Because such people do not reflect on the consequences of their actions, they do not have even the slightest bit of mindfulness about whether or not their actions harm others. What happens if we fall into this narrow way of thinking? Not only do we commit many negative actions that will ripen as negative or dark circumstances in the future, but we also become completely consumed by worldly life. We lose any chance at having spiritual lives because our self-cherishing occupies all the space within our hearts and minds. We are so full of ourselves that there is no room for anything or anyone else.

By now we have probably come to accept, at least at some level, that being self-consumed is what has been making us miserable all along. But by relying upon lojong training as our friend, we can be sure to cease living from this place. Protected by the armor of mindfulness and patience, we need not become so overwhelmed by ordinary life and the drive to get what we want in the future that we shatter our commitment to spiritual practice.

For those of us with even the smallest amount of spiritual inclination, falling into the mind-set of the mere human life is a devastating waste of time. It is a waste of our human heart and our human intelligence. Imagine what it feels like to fall into this shroud of darkness. Day in and day out, we spend our time and energy running through the rat hole of ordinary life without even a glimmer of hope that anything could ever be any different. We lack inspiration and motivation to grow and change. Living without any inspiration can destroy the natural goodness of the human heart. Take a moment to reflect on how many human beings are alive on the planet right now, and how many of them are living a mere human life. Most people alive in the world today are living like this, caught up in the struggle for mere survival, cloaked in feelings of fear, hopelessness, and unhappiness. Generate within yourself the motivation to abandon this narrow way of thinking from now on and to appreciate the circumstances you have.

The Adequate Human Life

According to Longchenpa, the majority of modern spiritual practitioners fall into the category of using their human lives for an adequate purpose. Longchenpa explains that many practitioners enter the path of the dharma and even put some effort into spiritual practice, but their motivations, thoughts, and actions are a mixture of black and white; they are both wholesome and nonwholesome.

When we fall into this manner of living, what is it that causes us not to keep our focus on positive, altruistic actions? It is our lack of mind training. Without putting enough effort into practicing the lojong teachings, we are unable to sustain the wish to benefit others within the mind. Each time this motivation is lost, we are in danger of falling into self-cherishing and doing something that harms others. Or we may begin an action—for example, offering a meal to a friend—with a completely selfless motivation. We spend time and money cooking a delicious meal meant to delight. However, by the end of the meal we may have lost this motivation and even become annoyed with our friend for not enjoying or appreciating our effort enough. What started out as a perfect motivation becomes tinged with selfishness.

Although perhaps we are not as mindless as those beings who are living a mere human life, we are unable to sustain our practice for a long period of time. As practitioners of lojong we can use the following analogy to guide us in our practice. The effort necessary to train the mind is like runners training for a marathon. When runners train for a marathon, their training is long and continuous, free of breaks and sustained periods of rest. They aim to achieve the endurance to run any course, no matter how difficult the challenge. Often marathon runners train on courses that are much more challenging or longer than those of the actual race they plan to enter. The result is that they become incredibly patient with all the challenging circumstances they meet on the road. They become free of fatigue and exhaustion.

Our mind training needs to reach the level of patience and endurance achieved by marathon runners if we are to remain constantly focused on the dharma. When we fail to reach this level of training we are distracted by our self-cherishing and all its expressions. At times, we drop the dharma and focus on our attachment toward ordinary life, our likes and dislikes, and our wants and needs. Longchenpa calls this being *enveloped in the busyness of ordinary life*. This distraction of ordinary life, in turn, causes us to continue acting out patterns that we know always result in unhappiness.

The Precious Human Life

Longchenpa defines a *precious human life* in the following way:

> A supreme practitioner who is a stainless vessel for
>   the dharma
> Masters listening and contemplation, and practices
>   the essential meaning.
> Applying these three, they tame themselves
> And also guide others in the way of virtue.

Many of the qualities of lojong practice are apparent in Long-chenpa's words. The word *masters* indicates a high level of mind training. Someone who is a master of listening, contemplation, and meditation must have deeply engaged in these activities so that they become deeply engrained and effortless. When we work with mind training, our goal is to overcome all the ordinary habits of the mind, especially our self-cherishing. Only by taking our practice to the level of mastery will this be possible. The word *applying* is also related to the practice of lojong. If we simply *listen* to the lojong teachings, or even reflect on them, but do not apply them, we will find it impossible to transform ourselves. We'll be just as miserable as before. However, when we apply the meaning of the teachings to ourselves, we are able to start embodying qualities such as loving-kindness, compassion, selflessness, patience, and altruism. The warm energy of this state of mind is the source of peace and well-being.

Listening to, contemplating, and meditating upon the dharma leads us along the path of genuine success. This is not worldly success, which is rewarded by fame, admiration, money, or recognition. It is the success of shedding layers of unhappy energy, of becoming lighter, of feeling younger, and of becoming self-motivated to continue with our spiritual practice. Through vigorous mind training we begin to transform ourselves. Our example either directly or indirectly encourages others to go beyond their mere worldly aspirations. We have all probably had times in which we wished we knew the best way to help the people we love. When we apply the lojong teachings to ourselves, we find the key to helping ourselves and others. As we begin to shed our own negative patterns and become more at ease with what we have and who we are, we emulate this example for others. We have the ability to inspire.

The Impermanence of This Precious Human Life

Even though we may have discovered the richness and possibility of this precious human life, if we forget its fleeting and momentary nature we may lose the chance to transform ourselves and to find a happier and more peaceful way to live. We lose the feeling of urgency to train the mind.

In previous chapters, we reflected broadly on the practice of impermanence. We broke down this human body into its constituent parts, the five aggregates. We used the *Heart Sutra* to reflect on the emptiness of the corporeal body and the mind itself. However, deepening our understanding of impermanence can further help us relax our grip on this body that we identify with as "me."

Reflecting on the impermanence of the human body, life, and the entire phenomenal world is one of the *four thoughts that turn the mind toward the dharma*. This phrase highlights the importance of training the mind in the impermanent nature of everything. If we do not become thoroughly convinced that everything around us—including ourselves, our identities, our emotions, our personalities, and our bodies—is impermanent, we will not turn toward the dharma. We will lose our focus and fall into the ravine of self-centeredness. We will resume our normal belief that going after what we want, rejecting what we dislike, and distinguishing between friends and enemies will bring us happiness.

The general Buddhist teachings present the nature of impermanence in a very sound and logical way. They discuss the impermanence of the phenomenal world, as evidenced by the changing seasons, the changing landscape of mountains and oceans, and the destruction of the empires and palaces of ancient powerful rulers. They also discuss the impermanence of the individual person, as evidenced by changing appearances, aging, illness, and death. Most of us read these explanations and genuinely feel that we understand the nature of impermanence. After all, we are educated, intelligent people. The impermanence of life is not a difficult concept to master. However, when facing something difficult, such as falling out with a friend or loved one, or the loss of a job, do we turn our minds toward the dharma in that moment?

What is my first instinct? Do I follow an old pattern, one that I know will bring me misery sooner or later? Or do I apply the dharma? How long does it take me to remember my spiritual practice? Once I remember it, am I willing to apply it?

When we reflect in this way, we can see that most of the time, our minds have not really turned toward the dharma. When times get tough, we go back to our old ways of doing things, just like that crooked stick. We may understand the nature of impermanence in an intellectual way, but we have not taken it deeper. If we emotionally accept the nature of impermanence, we will feel a sense of relief when things are most difficult. We'll think, *Of course this happened. It is impossible for things to remain the way they were. And in time, change will come again.* If we truly accept that everything is changing moment by moment, we won't be derailed when things do not go our way. If we really wish to master the lojong teachings, then further mind training is essential. To help us further train the mind in the impermanent nature of life, we can reflect on teachings of the certainty of death, which are presented in seven parts by the omniscient Longchenpa.

First, Contemplate the
Insubstantiality of the Body

All our self-cherishing, personal identities, and strong emotions originate in the body. So the very first thing we need to do is reflect on the body's insubstantial nature. We may want to think clearly about the meaning of the word *insubstantial* itself. Insubstantiality implies a lack of solidity and strength, and also a lack of reality. A third meaning of this word is to lack importance. When we apply this word to the physical body, we find that it is insubstantial in all three of these ways.

How do we recognize the body's lack of solidity and strength? We can notice how the body is constantly changing. From moment to moment we feel physical, mental, emotional, and energetic changes. We feel good, and then without reason we feel tired, agitated, hungry, or thirsty. One minute the sun feels good on our back, the next we feel the sensation of burning. The physical body is changeable and unpredictable. We cannot count on feeling any certain way consistently.

How do we understand the body's lack of reality? As we have already discussed, the body is completely empty of any lasting and permanent character. The body is completely empty of any nature, of being this or that. The body is a mishmash of parts and systems that work together to make it seem like a "whole."

How do we understand the body's lack of importance? Such an idea is contrary to our ordinary way of thinking. It is something that can only be accomplished through lojong practice. Without making a focused effort to place less importance on our physical selves, we will not be able to reduce the cherishing we have toward the body. Since the body is ever changing and empty of any lasting nature, just how important is it to protect ourselves and respond to every impulse that arises inside of us? For example, we may feel physically uncomfortable being in a new situation, such as visiting a dharma center where we do not practice regularly. If we respond to that feeling of discomfort by shutting down or leaving without talking to anyone, we will likely lose the chance to connect with what might be a wonderful support for our spiritual practice. Or if we feel physically sick and this physical feeling causes us to act aggressively toward a loved one, we will have to experience the suffering of that conflict on top of the illness we are already suffering from. In both cases, if we placed less importance on the body, we would achieve greater peace of mind. We would also gain the gift of positive connections and circumstances as support.

In the *Sutra Requested by a King*, the Buddha Shakyamuni teaches on this very topic, saying that the physical body will encounter four great catastrophes: birth, old age, sickness, and death. These four are called catastrophes because they are destructive and unavoidable—no matter how quick we are, we cannot escape them; no matter how strong we are, we cannot reverse them; no matter how rich we are, we cannot buy them off; no matter what kind of spiritual or ordinary powers we have, we cannot turn away from them. When old age comes, our strength begins to decline. The elements fall out of balance. We face all sorts of difficulty and suffering. Sickness doesn't necessarily come with old age, but it is another cause for a decline in strength whenever it occurs. Not being able to do the things that we did earlier in life is a cause of great physical, mental, and emotional suffering. When we experience old age and sickness, there is no escape. Degradation, decay, and decline are realities of life.

Whatever possessions we have, whatever abundance there is around us, will at some point be lost. We can reflect on not only losing our wealth but also on the even greater suffering some people incur, such as refugees who lose their countries, their homes, and their families. Even America, which was once the pinnacle of success, has experienced a gradual decline in its prosperity. This kind of loss will be experienced by all of us. It is one of the great catastrophes of this life.

For all of us without exception, life is followed by death. When we reflect on the certainty of death, we should reflect on the fundamental goal of our self-cherishing. We cherish ourselves to keep ourselves alive, to make ourselves comfortable so that we can avoid the certainty of what is to come. But no matter how much we cling to the lives that we have and the things that we think we need to survive, death will come to us all. Thinking *There has never been a person who has ever escaped from decay and death*, we can train the mind in the knowledge that the body we cherish is completely insubstantial.

Second, Contemplate the Limitations of Spiritual Power

Even the great spiritual masters experienced the insubstantiality of life. Some of us may fantasize that our spiritual practice will help us transcend the ordinary experiences of life and death. But such a transcendence has never happened for anyone on the planet who has come before us, no matter how masterful or realized they were. In reality, spiritual practice gives us the tools to help us relax and cope with the dangers and disasters still to come in life—illness, loss, separation, change, decline, and death. If we have the expectation that we are going to avoid the great catastrophe of death as a result of our spiritual practice, we should think again. This is likely the arising of our self-cherishing and our ego, which is always interested in its own preservation at the expense of the truth.

Third, Contemplate the Insubstantial Nature of Everything

No matter where we look, we cannot find anything that is a singular whole, meaning something that is not made up of constituent parts. If we examine every animal and insect, and all phenomena in the world, such as mountains, rocks, trees, flowers, buildings, cars, and even the contents of a coffee cup, none are beyond the impermanent and insubstantial nature of life. We can challenge ourselves to find something in our lives or our environment that seems lasting and permanent, and then notice the way its wholeness falls apart upon closer examination. How do we do this? We can reflect on all the causes and conditions that came together to make the appearance of wholeness before us. The myriad parts of everything are even smaller than what we can see. Even tiny particles such as atoms are made up of even tinier particles such as neutrons, electrons, and protons. We're of this same nature.

Fourth, Contemplate the Impermanence of the Lineage Masters

All the great Buddhist masters of the past, present, and future have experienced death or will experience it when their time comes. Even the Buddha Shakyamuni, the buddha of this modern age, could not avoid the experience of death. In the Buddhist tradition, we refer to the passing of Buddha Shakyamuni as one of his enlightened activities. This is because he used his death to teach others that life is fleeting, and to illustrate that spiritual practice must be done now, during our lifetimes, while we are still healthy.

No matter which Buddhist master we think of, all of them were impermanent. The arhats of the Theravada tradition; the bodhisattvas of the Mahayana tradition; the lineage masters of the Secret Mantrayana, starting with Garab Dorje and Manjushrimitra all the way down to Padmasambhava; and the later masters of the Longchen Nyinthig lineage such as Longchenpa, Jigme Lingpa, Patrul Rinpoche, and others—they were all expressions of impermanence. When the time came for their lives to end, they each dissolved into light like rainbows fading into the sky.

All the Kadampa masters of old such as Jowo Je Atisha, Geshe Ben, Shantideva, and Gyalsé Togmé Zangpo, whose advice we have been relying upon to skillfully take up the lojong teachings, also passed away when it was their time. When we reflect on all these great spiritual masters, we can only talk about them in past tense. We can say, "They were here, they lived in this way, they displayed this enlightened activity, they spoke these words . . ." but we cannot meet them in the flesh. How could we be any different?

We can also use our reflection on the fleeting lives of the spiritual masters as an opportunity to connect more deeply with living masters of our spiritual tradition. If we do not waste the chance that we have now to connect with spiritual masters, listen to their advice, and put it into practice, we will have taken a step closer to taking hold of this precious human life.

Fifth, Contemplate How Life Only Gets Shorter

The length of our lives can never be increased. Our lives are not like rain filling a depleted riverbed—appearing full again after a period of dryness. Our lives are only getting shorter with each passing day. Death is a certainty for us. The only things that are uncertain are how, where, and when we will die.

Reflect on how life is as ephemeral as water evaporating from a pond. Because we are mindless and forget this, we constantly procrastinate. We put off spiritual practice, thinking there will be a better time to work on it later. We have so many ideas about what we should be doing instead of training the mind and engaging in spiritual practice. Sometimes we are enticed by what we consider to be important life events, such as marriage or having children. We think these things are the key to happiness, so we dive into them without a second thought. We may think, *Right now I'm busy getting married. After I settle down, I'll make time to practice.* Or we may think that we will start practicing once our children get older, or once they leave for college and we have more free time. We may think that retirement gives us the greatest promise of time for spiritual practice, so we work hard now to save money for that distant day. No matter who we are, each and every one of us has used the wishes we have for happiness as an excuse to put aside dharma practice. The beauty of lojong practice is that it can be applied continuously, each moment, wherever we are, whatever we are doing. There is no need to procrastinate or wait for perfect circumstances that may never come. We can apply lojong training at any moment.

Forgetting that our lives are only getting shorter, we also use our present circumstances to put off the practice of the dharma. We might think that we need a vacation, and that this is more important than practice. Or we might think, *My body needs more rest . . . I'm not healthy enough to focus on practice.* Some of us even belong to spiritual communities but have trouble making the effort to show up for weekly or daily practice. Or we may feel that we are too young to get serious about spiritual practice, thinking that when we are young we should enjoy ourselves. Or we may feel that we are too old to be able to change substantially, so trying to apply spiritual practice to our long-ingrained habits isn't really worth it. But what other good choices do we have? As Longchenpa says, since life is uncertain, it is best to put aside the habit of procrastination.

When we hear a commercial or see an advertisement on television or in the newspaper promising a way to help us look younger, feel better, be more relaxed, or be happier, we can reflect on how we are constantly seeking the possibility of escape from the suffering of this big world we live in. But there is no escape from loss and death. When we reflect on the brevity of life, thinking that we are moving closer to death with each passing day, we may think to ourselves, *Yes, everything is impermanent. Yes, when I face the moment of death, I can't take any of it with me.* But the moment someone tries to get us to buy into the idea of the happiness of ordinary life, we jump at the chance of believing it. We are often willing to do things that we know will bring us pain or difficulty in the future because we so desperately want to believe it.

We may know that life is impermanent and insubstantial, but we are still shrouded by thought patterns that tell us that we can find happiness if we arrange our lives just so. We fail to realize that the moments passing by can never be reclaimed. Day by day we grow older and are in danger of losing our health. Have we considered how much more difficult it will be to practice if we become seriously ill or in physical pain, and as we experience a decline in heath due to aging? Instead we obsess about what could be, "if only." If we can just get rid of this unwanted circumstance, that unwanted person, that intolerable emotional habit . . . sooner or later we will find happiness. To be more specific, the main problem we have is that we believe we can find happiness outside of our spiritual practice, outside of ourselves. We may have the thought to engage in lojong practice for a time, but the moment we drop it we are again mired in habits that cause us to believe that sooner or later the way we always do things will bring us good results. We are invested in living out these ideas and patterns that we have always had, thinking, *It didn't work well the last time but definitely this time I'm going to find happiness.* Even if we are not thinking this way consciously, we are living this way all the time.

Sixth, Contemplate the Impermanence of Loved Ones

Our friends, spouses, family members, and communities are all impermanent. We can be certain that we will have to separate from every single person we love sooner or later. Not only will we separate from every person we love but also those we are merely connected to and those we dislike. We should have no doubt about this. When we look to the world outside, we can see that this is true in every case. We may separate from loved ones because of death, accidents, or discord. Some spouses are widowed after fifty years of marriage. But even spouses who start out loving each other deeply can have conflicts that end in divorce. Brothers and sisters who grow up in the same house may become estranged or turn against one another. There is no permanent or lasting relationship. Change is imminent. Even if we maintain a strong and intimate connection with someone for our whole lives, we will still have to leave that person behind at the time of death.

During our lifetimes, we have this mistaken idea that our enemies are our greatest obstacles, but our greatest obstacles are the people we cherish the most. Because of our attachment, we suffer when we face change and loss. We avoid the realities of life. In doing so, we fall down, and sometimes we do not know how to pick ourselves up.

Seventh, Take up Contemplation as a Daily Practice

Longchenpa's final instruction emphasizes the practice of lojong. Many of us may reflect on the impermanent nature of life from time to time. But without making this style of contemplation a central focus of our practice, how will we turn the mind toward the dharma when we need it most? We are sure to continue on just the way we always have. Take a moment to think of the mental and emotional patterns we have already and how deeply ingrained they are. Imagine what kind of strength we need to dig them up, smooth them over, and rid ourselves of them completely. But along with the precious human life, we have also met with the one thing we need most to liberate ourselves from the cycle of suffering. We have encountered the dharma and found lojong, the key to our freedom. Lojong gives us the great opportunity to use each and every circumstance we encounter on a daily basis as a means to turn our minds toward the dharma.

Whether the situations we meet with are happy or unhappy, we can remind ourselves, *This situation is bound to change*. Whether we feel a sense of elation or misery within the mind, we can think, *My feelings change moment by moment*. When we leave a place, we should think, *I may never return here*. When we eat a meal, we should think, *This may be the last time I eat*. When we go to sleep at night, we should think, like the great Kadampa masters of old, *I may never wake again*. Armed with the knowledge that we have only the lives that we have at this moment, with no guarantee of anything in the future, we have every reason to make the most of it and invest all our energy in personal change for the well-being of ourselves and others.

7

Lojong and the Vajrayana Vehicle

M ANY OF THE lojong techniques that we have been discussing are contemplative in nature and thus have a subtle
yet profound effect over time. In other words, when we reflect on
larger ideas such as the nature of friends and enemies, the nature
of self-cherishing, the five aggregates, the precious human life,
and the insubstantial nature of everything, our attitudes undergo
a gradual shift. As we put more and more energy into these new
ideas, slowly a new way of thinking dawns in us. As we discussed
in chapter 6, this shift away from ourselves, our wants, and needs
toward others helps us turn ourselves toward the dharma. Over
the course of our lifetimes, even this gradual shift in thinking
will be enough to kindle a radical transformation within us, not
unlike the radical thoughts, beliefs, and actions of the lojong
masters of old.

Although in the long run this shift will be extremely helpful,
it may not bring us immediate relief from the strong emotional
patterns we are feeling right now. This is analogous to the way
that pouring a cup of water on a raging fire will not douse the
flames. Although the water can lower the intensity of the fire for
an instant, it is burning much too hot to be put out by this small
quantity of water. Let's put this back in terms of our emotions.
If we become completely enraged and then attempt to reflect on

the nature of the five aggregates as a way to control or deflate our anger, this intellectual contemplation will not have the power to diffuse the intense energy inside of us. It is more likely that we will have to wait for some time for the emotional energy in our bodies and minds to calm down. Why is this? It is because we have waited so long to apply our lojong practice that our habits are ingrained in us. We have let the energy of our emotions build unchecked, and they have taken on lives of their own.

If we refuse or are unable to let go of our strong emotions, gradually the energy of those emotions will wear itself into us, the same way repeated footsteps wear a path into the hillside. Over time, the emotional responses we repeat the most will become part of our basic energy pattern. For example, if we generate a feeling of intense anger that we are truly unwilling to let go of over a period of time, it will harden as resentment, and we will carry it with us for the long haul.

In the brief time that we have been alive, all kinds of heavy energy patterns have worn themselves into our bodies and minds. We experience them as triggers and vulnerabilities—our most sensitive points. When we allow strong emotions to build unchecked again and again, right on top of these triggers, we could say that they almost become hardened within us. The result is that they become more and more difficult to release.

We often refer to these hardened emotions that we are unwilling to let go of as our emotional baggage. Even though the phrase "emotional baggage" has a negative connotation in our language, many times we do not realize that we are the main contributors to this heavy load we are carrying. Perhaps we are unwilling or unable to see our emotions for what they are and to make the effort to eradicate them. Or maybe we think we can carry these patterns with us for the time being and get rid of them later, not realizing that the longer we leave them to their own devices, the more difficult it is to purify our hardened and heavy emotional patterns.

If we are honest with ourselves, we will find that even the heaviest parts of our emotional baggage started with the feeling that our emotions are justified and necessary, and with an unwillingness to let go of certain emotional responses. This statement is not meant to cause us to fall into feelings of self-judgment. When we think back over our lives, even to our most painful and vulnerable experiences, strong emotional responses may have been warranted by some of the situations we faced. For example, if we experienced a situation where someone we knew and trusted inflicted physical or emotional harm upon us, having a fearful memory of that situation is nothing to feel bad about. But the question we should ask ourselves now is whether or not we want to continue putting energy into that situation that happened so long ago, or whether we are willing to turn the mind away from it and toward the dharma.

In the current lives we are living, we all feel that a certain level of emotional response is acceptable. When it comes to these acceptable emotions, we are not willing to let go of them. We might take some time to examine whether or not this statement is true. After having spent much time thinking about how much suffering our self-cherishing and emotions bring us, it may seem illogical for us to think that there are emotions that we do not want to let go of. After all, we often feel that we are trying as hard as we can to change. We know our emotional patterns are causing us a great deal of pain, and we feel desperate to let them go. But ironically, we still love our emotions in spite of the fact that they cause us to suffer. We keep them close and dialogue with them as we process information and think about what to do next.

Let's put this idea into context. What if our best friend betrays our confidence and tells something personal and shameful to a person whom we do not trust? Most of us are sure to have some kind of emotional reaction to this sort of situation. In the beginning we may feel justified in our feelings of betrayal, mistrust, and anger. After all, our friend should have been loyal to us. They should not have exposed our weakness, especially to someone we dislike. Because our friend has unexpectedly done us wrong, we think that we deserve to feel hurt. And during this time when we feel upset and hurt, we may not even feel it is needed or desirable to let go of our emotions. Our feelings keep us company while we figure out how to handle the situation.

When we are relating to our emotions as friends and personal confidants in this way, we may not be able to turn genuinely toward the dharma. This is because at this stage in our emotional process, we do not have the goal of releasing whatever feelings have arisen. When we are caught up in our emotional response, how could we possibly put the genuine dharma into practice? Rather, we should realize that we have welcomed the emotional response that we are having into our bodies, hearts, and minds. Whenever we refuse to apply lojong practice to our emotions, we are engaging in self-cherishing. Again, we need not judge ourselves for doing this. But we should also realize that sooner or later self-cherishing will make it so that we will be the cause of our own unhappiness.

When we are in the midst of relating to our emotions as friends, they seem to serve some positive purpose. They seem to be doing us more good than harm. But if we extend our vision and think more long-term, we can see what will happen if we are unwilling or unable to let go of these feelings that seem perfectly acceptable to us now. The feelings of betrayal, anger, and mistrust will grow. The movement of these feelings through body and mind will cause a shift in our mood and energy. This will affect our eating, sleeping, and how we feel throughout the day.

We are also likely to engage in all kinds of behavior that causes us even more unhappiness. For example, we may stop trusting this one friend, and we may also extend this feeling of mistrust to everyone around us. We may withdraw, feel anxious or depressed, or disconnect from others. Even if we avoid disconnecting, the energy of this emotion will still affect our moods, physical bodies, energy, demeanor, and gestures. We may feel uncomfortable in our own bodies, which will make others also feel uncomfortable around us. Only when our emotions reach this level—when we no longer feel we are enjoying their protection but rather we are under their control—can we finally see their true faces.

Many of us are incredibly sensitive toward the energy of the places we visit and the people we meet. The moment we enter a room, we notice whether we feel comfortable or uncomfortable. We notice if the atmosphere is heavy or light, if it makes us feel anxious or relaxed. We notice the subtle feelings within the body that seem to arise based on what is going on around us and how the people and places we encounter affect our mood. But do we notice how our own emotional energy affects ourselves and others? For example, how do our bodies feel when they sustain patterns of sadness, depression, anxiety, anger, or resentment over a long period of time? Perhaps we feel heavy and unmotivated, as we become exhausted by our own emotions. Perhaps we feel tense and anxious, and relate to others with a sense of impatience, mistrust, and fear. Have we taken time to think about how our energy affects the people we encounter? Have we ever considered how our energy colors the feeling in a room? If we are people who wish to serve others and bring them happiness, this is something we need to pay attention to. After all, our practice of bodhichitta is not limited to what we say and do. It is also related to the sense of peace, warmth, or relief that we can offer others.

Having contemplated the lojong teachings at length, we are now at a crossroads. We have reached the point where we may want to run away. Even though we think we are open and receptive toward new ideas, we may not really want to hear what comes next. After all, it is going to threaten the very lives of our egos and self-cherishing. And if we truly understand how to practice lojong properly, it is going to take away the role of our emotions as our closest confidants.

The truth of the matter is that we are unable to control the shift that occurs between when our emotional responses are acceptable to us and when we recognize that they are self-destructive.

As practitioners of lojong, then, we must conclude that the only way to ensure that we're not going to have to face the misery and destruction of our strong emotions is by letting go of each and every emotion that arises, as quickly as we can. We do not have the luxury of choosing between which emotions protect us and are justified and which seem destructive and harmful. We do not get to decide how long we will hold on to certain emotions and when we will release them. We have been tricking ourselves into thinking this is something we are capable of. We have been playing this dangerous game with our emotions all along. When we have invited strong emotions into our minds and bodies, we have mistakenly believed that we would discard the emotions as soon as they had worn out their welcome. But if we are truly honest with ourselves, we have been stuck in certain emotions and driven by certain patterns for much longer than we would like to admit, and many times we have felt there was nothing we could do about it.

When we think of all the misery our emotions bring us, we should reflect on the situation seriously. *Why take the risk of getting stuck in an unhappy pattern this time? Why think that I will be able to get out of an emotion that has always defeated me in the past?*

What does this mean exactly? Rather than banking on the mistaken idea that we will be able to turn the energy of an emotional pattern around when we have never been able to do it before, a master of lojong realizes that it is wiser not to pick up the emotion in the first place. Not only that, but such a master also realizes that it is in his or her own self-interest to release each and every emotion that arises as quickly as possible, just as we would desperately attempt to remove the poison from the body when we are bitten by a rattlesnake.

Attempting to adopt this way of thinking can raise all kinds of questions in us. First of all, what about our best friend who betrayed us? How can we let this person off with no anger and no punishment? Why can't we be angry for a time, so that we can teach our friend to treat us better? But we should be clear that lojong is an extremely practical set of teachings. Lojong teachings are intended to show us the way to a happier and more peaceful state of mind. They are not concerned with the need to enforce negative consequences on others. They are not worried about making sure that others get what they deserve. As practitioners of lojong, we must be extremely pragmatic. Allowing others to experience the natural consequences of their actions is something that we will have to accept if we are to find peace of mind. Concerning ourselves with the consequences of others' actions gives rise to a state of mind that is resentful, angry, or wishes negativity on others, and that will only harm us in the end.

Simply put, to take up this practice seriously, we must realize that we are not in control of our emotions. Our emotions are in control of us. We are not capable of nurturing a strong emotional response for a time and then releasing it when we think it is no longer useful. It is actually the other way around. Our emotions are so strong that they can outlive our resolve to let them go. In order to release our emotional responses and reactions, we often go to battle—and lose. So as lojong practitioners, we resolve to go to battle with our emotions rather than with the people and situations whom we used to view as our enemies. We must be willing to work as hard and as long as necessary to break these emotions down so that we can be released from their grip entirely.

It is difficult to think about letting others off the hook when they hurt us. It can seem unfair and unjust not to respond in kind to someone who clearly deserves it. We should understand that this does not mean we can't make deliberate changes in our own behavior when such changes are warranted. This does not mean that we think it is okay for others to act harmfully toward us, and that we do not take any action ourselves. However, the way that we respond to outer situations is based on the inner dialogue of the lojong teachings. For example, we might think, *If I invest my energy in being angry with my friend, I will lose the opportunity to practice the dharma. I will waste the opportunity I have to practice here and now, because I'm not capable of controlling the energy of anger. Also, if I invest my energy in being angry, I'm reinforcing my own self-cherishing, which is the true cause of my own unhappiness.* After reflecting in this way, we can choose to act in a way that is warranted by the situation but has no emotional charge behind it. If we wish to give everything that we have to spiritual practice, then by reflecting in this way, we can see that when we react with anger, we hurt ourselves.

This is the true difference between practitioners of lojong and ordinary people. Practitioners of lojong focus wholly on the goal of releasing emotional responses because they know that sooner or later their own responses will cause their own suffering. Practitioners of lojong are not concerned with the appearance of fairness and justice. Recall the example of Patrul Rinpoche, who dressed as a beggar and was unconcerned with being treated with respect and kindness when he was able to benefit the deceased. Recall the example of Geshe Ben, who saw his wish to get his own share of yogurt as his true enemy.

Finding Relief from Strong Emotions

In order to bring ourselves relief from our strong emotions, we must leave no method untried and no stone unturned. Our emotional habits are seductive and slippery, like thieves lying in wait. Even though we may think that we are practicing the dharma diligently and engaging in the techniques of lojong to really transform our entire approach to living, the moment we let down our guard those emotions pop right back up.

By working with the general lojong teachings, we have already developed many of the tools that we need to tame our strong emotions. However, the tradition of the Secret Mantrayana, a special set of teachings found within the Nyingma lineage of Vajrayana Buddhism, contains extremely effective means for releasing strong emotions in the moment. However, all the methods contained within the Secret Mantrayana begin by working with impermanence as their basis.

We discussed calling to mind the impermanence of life and our bodies as a way to generally cut through self-cherishing. But here our discussion of impermanence takes on a different purpose. We want to firmly take hold of the teachings of impermanence so that we can apply them the moment strong emotions arise. Then, without discriminating between whether we think they are good and justified emotions or shameful and destructive emotions, we want to apply the antidote of impermanence to shorten the emotions' duration, to lessen their intensity, and to release the emotions' grasp on the mind.

Using Lojong to Develop Samadhi

From the point of view of the general Buddhist teachings, the entire phenomenal world including ourselves, other people and beings, and the outer phenomenal world are of an illusory or dreamlike nature. This is further elaborated upon in the Secret Mantrayana by the use of eight examples, which are the topic of the famous text *Resting in Illusory Nature*, composed by the omniscient Longchenpa. This text has introductory instructions for beginner practitioners, and it also has very advanced and profound instructions. A commentary on some, but not all, of those eight instructions has been included below.

We should recognize that these instructions are not just important for us, as beginning practitioners of lojong. They're of paramount importance to any genuine practitioner of the dharma—so important that Longchenpa devotes an entire text to explaining how to put them into practice. If we had to distill the meaning of this text to its main essence, we could say that by applying these eight examples of illusory nature diligently, on a moment-by-moment basis, all our attachment, confusion, fears, hopes, and doubts will naturally dissolve.

Longchenpa's teachings are based on the idea that engaging in mind training can help us develop the quality of samadhi. *Samadhi* (Tib. *teng nge zin*) is a word that describes the state in which meditation has been absorbed by the mind, such that mind and meditation have become indivisible. Another way to understand the word *samadhi* is by describing it as "one-pointedness." When the mind is undistracted and one-pointedly focused on a contemplative idea or practical technique, nothing else has the opportunity to arise within the mind. Practice is the sole focus.

When we reflect on the manner of using the examples of impermanence below, we should understand the goal as being to develop one-pointedness toward whichever example we are working with. For example, if we are working with the first example, "everything is the nature of a dream," then our goal is to focus on this idea so much that no matter what occurs within or without us, we are not swayed by it. Even if the sky is falling or our deepest beliefs are shattered, we are so bound to the dreamlike nature of everything that it begins to bleed through and influence our experience of whatever is happening. When this happens, we begin to breathe and slowly relax, even in the face of intense difficulty.

Reflect on the Dreamlike Nature of Everything

Not only ourselves and all outer phenomena, but our feelings, moods, physical and emotional energy—all of it is like a dream. All of it is an illusion. Because we all experience the dream state when we sleep at night, it is easy for us to understand the illusory nature of everything in this way. We truly believe that the dream state is real when it appears before us, but as soon as we awaken, we realize that it was nothing more than an illusion. Even if we awaken in terror, our fear diminishes as soon as we realize there was never anything to be afraid of in the first place.

Our dreams are filled with emotionally charged situations, and we feel the full force of our emotions as we face the varying situations that appear before us while we sleep. When we have nightmares, our hearts race as though we are truly in danger. When we become infuriated in dreams, we may wake up with the taste and feeling of anger still in our chests. But we soon realize that although our dreamtime emotions were vivid, their causes were nothing more than illusions. Nothing actually happened.

It is easy to see that the emotions we have in dreams are based on all sorts of unreal conditions; they're simply the mind acting out its own well-worn patterns. But treating the emotions we have while we are awake in this same manner can be a challenge. When we face an emotionally charged situation, such as when someone we love is in a car accident, we may not be able to think that either the situation or our reaction to it is nothing more than an illusion, a dream. However, if we're able to apply this metaphor to both the situation as well as to the emotions arising in our minds, we will find the calm and clarity to deal with the situation. Even if there is nothing we can do to make things better immediately, there is certainly nothing to be gained by getting upset.

In the beginning, we may find it easier to reflect on life situations as being illusory in nature rather than our personal inner world. Our lives often have a dreamlike quality. When we face something unexpected or unwanted, the events happening around us can seem unbelievable and unreal. We may find it easier to apply this metaphor to outer situations as we go throughout our day, to help cultivate our one-pointed samadhi. No matter what we see—a crowd on the street, a family walking in the park, a traffic accident, a picnic table set with a beautiful meal—all of it is like a dream. No matter what is appearing around us we can think to ourselves that these appearances are just like the dreams we have at night.

The nature of ordinary life is like a dream. As we have already discussed in earlier chapters, everything is composed of the nature of the five aggregates. There is nothing real, lasting, and permanent—not even ourselves. Even our sensory perceptions are dreamlike. If we can begin to apply this metaphor over and over again throughout the day, for many days in succession, a change is certain to dawn in the mind. No matter what we see, hear, smell, taste, or touch, we will begin to hesitate before we fully jump into the experience, throwing caution to the wind, when we understand its dreamlike nature. We will slow down our own ordinary judgments and assessments of life situations and emotions. As a result, we will begin to realize that the more we grasp on to the reality of the phenomenal world, as well as our bodies and minds, the stronger our emotions will be.

When we begin to feel some hesitancy about fully diving into our own cognitive and emotional perceptions, we will naturally begin to apply this metaphor to the mind itself. When we encounter something painful, we might have two different responses at the same time. First, we might begin to feel our ordinary emotional reactions pop up. But within the mind, in that moment we hesitate to dive into that experience, we might also have a moment where we realize the situation may not be the way we think it is. If we see the illusory nature of the emotions that arise, even for a moment, we may be able to temper the emotional patterns that arise. We may be able to soften our reactions or the way we interact with the situation. We may be able to change our response to one that invites less pain and suffering for us in the future.

To begin to temper and unravel our emotional responses, we must be able to apply this style of lojong practice to any movement of the mind, no matter what emotions arise. We must apply it equally to any afflictive emotions that arise, even when we feel our emotions are justified, that we have been wronged, or that we need to protect ourselves. These habits of self-cherishing must be completely done away with if we are to succeed in this style of practice. Attachment, anger, ignorance, pride, jealousy, and all their various expressions are of the illusory nature of a dream, and we must treat them as just that.

Think about the benefit of training in samadhi based on recognizing that everything is of an illusory nature. If we one-pointedly train in the idea that all is of the nature of a dream, then our sense of "I" begins to dissolve. If we reflect on the fact that the four elements of earth, water, fire, and air are of the nature of a dream, this reduces our grasping at the phenomenal world. If we reflect on ourselves, our experiences, our feelings, and our perceptions as being dreamlike, our very beings will begin to relax and soften in response to that reflection. We will find that we need not invest so much energy and aggression in protecting and defending ourselves. There is more space within the heart and mind for happiness and joy because we're not filled with as many intense feelings, ideas, and perceptions. We are freer to let some things go. Over time, we are willing to let more and more things go.

We may wonder, *Will I still be okay? Won't others take advantage of me?* But we will feel so relaxed and supported by our own stability of mind that we will begin to not put much stock in these kinds of thoughts. Instead we will realize that part of the price of happiness is letting go of the habit of keeping score.

One very special piece of advice that Longchenpa gives is to forget yesterday's suffering just like last night's dream. Think how much happier we would be if we could follow this advice. When we first encounter a painful situation, the sting can be so intense that it is almost unbearable. This is just like when we awaken in the morning after having a terribly vivid dream about something important to us. Perhaps we witnessed our beloved embracing another person lovingly and we awaken with feelings of jealousy, betrayal, hurt, and anger in our body and mind. But slowly, through the course of the day, the appearances of the dream are forgotten. We forget the sequence of events, the places we saw, the people we met, and what happened. Later we may recall the main storyline of the dream, but it no longer seems real. Finally we may forget it completely. If we treat all of yesterday's suffering just like this, not grasping at it or investing energy into it to keep it alive, we will surely have a great deal of peace within the heart and mind.

Once we are able to forget yesterday's suffering like last night's dream, we can apply this same technique to tomorrow's suffering, and also to the suffering we are experiencing right now. Imagine the imprint of suffering fading from the mind just like a rainbow in the sky.

A Note of Caution

Before we continue with Longchenpa's instructions, we should all reflect on the importance of cultivating and maintaining our bodhichitta. When we begin to engage in authentic Vajrayana practice, there can be a tendency among modern practitioners to do away with their focus on loving-kindness, compassion, and bodhichitta, and only focus on developing this aspect of wisdom in their meditation. However, if we do this, we will never make any progress on the Vajrayana path. Vajrayana is a Buddhist tradition whose very foundation joins compassion and wisdom. To practice wisdom without compassion is, frankly speaking, not to practice wisdom at all.

How could this division manifest in our practice? We might begin to feel judgmental or dismissive toward others when we witness their struggles. We might think, *Since everything is of the nature of a dream, why do they have to be so upset?* In other words, we might use our practice to become even more selfish, impatient, and cold. If we notice this tendency beginning to arise within us, we should be sure to turn it around as soon as we can. Although we are watchful of our minds and emotional patterns, we should remain loving, warm, and patient with others. We should do our best to offer an ear generously when needed, and to do whatever we can to help others find happiness and peace of mind.

Contemplate the Nature of Everything as a Magician's Illusion

Just as we were contemplating everything as being of the nature of a dream, we can also train the mind to recognize everything as being like a magician's trick. How do we do this? When a magician creates an illusion, he or she is aware of exactly how the illusion is conjured and what is needed to create the effect. Every part of the illusion is planned beforehand, and the magician keeps mindful awareness of all the moving parts of the trick in order to make it display realistically. But for the observer, the magician's trick looks real, natural, and effortless. Because the observer does not know how the trick works, the illusion still appears to be real even if the observer is informed that it is indeed a trick. Only if the observer is taught all the elements of the trick can he or she properly see through it as an illusion.

In the face of our own emotions, we are just like that observer who believes everything he or she sees. We do not realize that our own minds, fueled by self-cherishing, are conjuring appearances, perceptions, and emotions at every moment. They look real; they seem trustworthy. But they are laden with the emotional patterns and perceptions that are our habits and biases. They encourage us to keep on reacting to situations and sensory objects in the same way that we have in the past. We are so close to our thoughts, feelings, and perceptions that it is hard to imagine that they are anything other than objective reality. If we could stare those thoughts, perceptions, and emotions straight in the eye without reacting to them, recognizing them to be just like the magician's trick, they would begin to loosen their grip on us.

Just as we do when we develop samadhi based on the dream-like nature of everything, we can also develop samadhi based upon recognizing that everything is like a magician's trick—a trick of our egos and self-cherishing. We can apply this way of thinking throughout our daily lives, building momentum with this practice so that eventually we are able to apply it to our emotions and perceptions in order to slowly undo them.

Contemplate the Nature of Everything as a Hallucination

We believe that the way we see things is infallible. We say, "Seeing is believing" or "I have to see it firsthand." We may not believe what someone else says, but if we have seen it firsthand, we believe that we can absolutely trust our perception. When we contemplate everything as having the nature of a hallucination, we challenge this way of thinking.

We tend to think that the difference between us and people who are either crazy or under the influence of drugs or alcohol is that *we* see things properly while they hallucinate—seeing, hearing, smelling, tasting, and touching things that are not really there. Ordinarily, people who are hallucinating completely believe their hallucinations. For example, if we encounter a person who believes she is standing on the edge of the ocean, no matter how you try to convince her that there is dry land in front of her, she will not step forward. Or if someone, out of paranoia, is convinced that we are out to get him, no matter what kindness we show, we will not be able to convince him otherwise.

As we discussed in earlier chapters, the nature of everything has no real, lasting essence. We cannot say exactly what is what.

When things are broken down into their constituent parts, their ordinary appearances crumble. When we think in this way, it is easy to see that the nature of everything is exactly like a hallucination. We may believe that we know the true nature of everything and that our way of seeing is infallible, but our perceptions are certainly colored by our cognitive and emotional patterns and are laden with dualistic vision.

We can train in the samadhi of seeing everything as the nature of a hallucination as we did in the examples of the dreamlike nature and the nature of the magician's trick. No matter what we encounter, whether it be in the outside world or an emotion or perception within the mind, we can question its very reality and our own accuracy, thereby slowly deflating the energy behind our perceptions.

Contemplate Everything as a Reflection of the Moon on Water

When we look at the reflection of the moon on the surface of a lake, the reflection is a mirror image of the moon in the sky. Because we are able to look up at the sky and see the actual moon, we know that the moon's reflection isn't really the moon. However, what would happen if we had never seen the moon in the sky? When we saw the reflection of the moon on water, we would mistake that reflection for the actual moon.

The nature of everything is just like the reflection of the moon on water. All phenomena—including ourselves, our bodies, our emotions, our perceptions, and our moods—appear yet are empty, having no real or lasting nature. Yet we believe them to be solid, permanent, and real. We can start to notice how when an emotion arises within the mind, it changes almost instantly. It may become weaker or stronger. It may give rise to thoughts that remind us of prior injury or resentment, which fuel even more emotions. The mind may become stuck, obsessing about that emotion over and over again. We may also notice that the arising of the emotions causes changes in our physical energy and our moods. We may begin to feel agitated, impulsive, or impatient. Our energy may become heavy or amplified. Any number of changes may come.

When we witness these changes to body, mind, mood, and emotions, we should reflect on how we're just like the reflection of the moon on water. We think of ourselves as being stable and dependable, but our emotions are unpredictable and change at whim as we react to different sensory objects. When we experience an intense emotion, we can directly see it as a mere reflection, something that appears but is not real, lasting, and permanent. We can use this way of thinking to awaken ourselves to the reality that we too are nothing more than the reflection of what we believe to be true about ourselves.

Find Stability in Samadhi

When we apply any of these metaphors, we can attempt to mingle them with our own thought patterns. No matter what happens and no matter how we feel about it, if we use those thoughts or feelings as a way to develop samadhi, we will notice a great acceleration in our mind training. By doing this we see the importance of applying lojong in a very specific way—to ourselves, our thoughts, and our emotions at each and every moment. We will need to rely upon a great deal of mindfulness to remember to apply any of these metaphors to strong emotions that arise within us. But if we come to the place where we are willing to apply lojong instead of keeping score, or worrying about what we and others deserve, we will have already won a great battle.

We may wonder why Longchenpa discusses more than one way to apply the same technique. The answer is that we relate to the teachings differently. Naturally we will find it easier to apply one metaphor than another because it fits us just right. Once we discover a technique that we are willing to apply in the moment, we should stick with it and apply it as often as we can. Gradually we will be able to apply lojong to our emotions more quickly and frequently.

8

Using Lojong to Release Old Patterns

THE IDEA of dropping emotions as soon as they arise is enticing. It is the very essence of the extremely profound path of the Secret Mantrayana and our special Longchen Nyingthig lineage. However, there are very few modern practitioners who properly understand how to do this. Most of us think that we are dropping our emotions when we are just chasing after them in a different way. This happens because our relationship with our emotions is very tricky. It is laden with so many complex layers of attachment. Also, since we have rarely—or perhaps never—experienced what it is like to release our emotions, we have no way of knowing when we are doing it right.

But it is really our attachment to the energy of the body that is paramount. Besides just relating to the emotions as close friends, confidants, or protectors, we also have intense and visceral attachments to the energetic patterns and even the subtle sensations of the emotions within the body. This is true when we consider a pleasant energetic pattern, such as the sensation of sensual pleasure, laughter, or elation. But this is also true when emotional patterns come up that we dislike. We identify with our basic energy patterns as "me" in the same way that we identify with strong emotions such as anger or jealousy or our roles as spouses, parents, or employees.

For example, when we feel a pattern of coldness or heaviness arise, we may have the wish to escape it immediately. But the moment that cold and heavy energy disappears, we are uncomfortable with the change. We become further agitated, just in a different way. Even though our energy is constantly fluctuating within the body, we have strong preferences toward feeling a certain way. It doesn't matter whether the energy pattern that we prefer actually feels good—we are attached to what we are used to. We are attached to identifying ourselves as "somebody" and using our emotions to fortify our identities.

When we begin to work earnestly with lojong practice, there will certainly be times when our practice makes us uncomfortable, as we enter uncharted waters. We are going to feel different. Sometimes we may feel tense with change. But other times we will feel ease and relaxation. No matter what kind of change it is, it may be difficult for us to handle, because we are all creatures of habit. Finding balance is something new to us. When we experience the spaciousness of our own minds, it can make us feel uncomfortable. In such moments we need to remember our lojong practice. Our energy, our essence, our very being—all of it is impermanent. Given some time, our physical and emotional energy is bound to change. If we watch the mind, we will notice this happening over and over again. Without any cause whatsoever, the mind will become agitated, and we will chase after it without a moment's hesitation simply because we are more comfortable that way.

We should not underestimate our attachment to the body's feelings, moods, and sensations. The relationship we have with the physical body is our most intimate connection. Up until now, we have been trying to appease our emotional patterns rather than purify and change them. We have let them be in control of our decisions as we simply followed suit, hoping that this would bring us relief. As we begin to turn everything we do, say, and feel upside down with our lojong practice, we may find that even we ourselves are resistant to the change. The emotional and energetic patterns that we have developed over the course of this lifetime are formidable. We are fighting with something deeply rooted within us.

Remember the saying "Happiness is hard to bear"? This saying points to the difficulty we face in trying to truly drop our emotional patterns in the moment. Although we all wish for happiness and believe that we are doing everything we can to find happiness, the moment we feel a sense of happiness, we feel uncomfortable and do something to chase the feeling away. The wise lojong master Shantideva says that although we human beings all wish for happiness, we chase it away like an enemy. If we are honest with ourselves, we have to admit the truth of this statement. We have buried the habit of feeling dissatisfied and unhappy deep inside. We may think that we truly want to cut ties with the strongest of our enemies, but the tendencies that have been building up inside of us are not easy to reverse.

Grasping, Attaching, and Pursuing

We can deepen our understanding of what it means to release emotions, habits, or energetic patterns on the spot by reflecting on what the omniscient Longchenpa describes as the threefold habit of the mind: grasping, attaching, and pursuing. Longchenpa explains that while we experience our attachment to feelings and experiences in a single instant, the attachment actually occurs in three stages. Grasping is our first reaction when we come in contact with energy patterns, moods, thoughts, or sensory objects. It is the mind's most innate habit to perceive dualistically; to grasp everything that we come in contact with as either "I" or "other." This is the supreme moment to release arising thoughts, emotions, or energy patterns.

Attachment is a stronger form of grasping. In the second stage, we attach more firmly to our experience. Habits are triggered, and reactions begin to reverberate in body and mind. Energy begins to rise and move within the body; respiration changes. The feelings intensify. It is harder to release thoughts, emotions, or energy patterns when we have already attached to them. Once patterns are triggered, the energy builds very quickly inside of us. It permeates our channels and moves throughout the body. At that point, sometimes watching the energy build only adds to the intensity of the feelings rather than helping release them.

Most of us do not even notice the first two stages of the mind's habit. They happen in an instant, and we are so unaware of what is happening within our own bodies and minds that we overlook them completely. But contemplating the third stage, pursuing, is especially illuminating for us. No matter what is happening, whether we like it or dislike it, when we are involved in our thinking and emotions, we are pursuing. We may not think we are pursuing, especially when it comes to feelings, thoughts, and memories of things that hurt us in the past or present. But this is the mind's fundamental habit.

No matter what we are thinking or feeling—even when we are reliving our most painful or terrifying experiences—we are pursuing. Of course, when we are reliving our happiest and most desirous moments, we are also pursuing. Even when we feel neutral and disinterested, we are pursuing. Until now we may have thought that we were just following the mind's ordinary habit to get caught up in our emotional energy patterns. But what Longchenpa says is stronger than this. We are not passively participating. We are actively pursuing our emotions, feeding them, and making them stronger on a moment-by-moment basis. We may not wish to do this, but it is part of the human condition.

If we begin to reflect often on the mind's basic tendency to pursue any experience, we can start to become aware of our self-cherishing at a deeper level. The mind's tendency to pursue is directly related to our sense of "I." Because we relate to ourselves as "me," we have a deep habit of chasing after and interpreting everything we see, feel, smell, taste, and touch. We can also contemplate the mind's basic tendency to grasp to help us see ourselves better. As we have already noticed, we think we want to be rid of our negative habits and painful emotions. We think that we want to change, that we are willing to change. But our minds are chasing after our experiences and emotions with such great speed and efficiency. No ordinary willingness or resolve is going to be enough to undo this fundamental habit of the mind.

This is why the Secret Mantrayana presents a special set of teachings within the cycle of teachings known as *Atiyoga* that can be practiced by extremely diligent, dedicated, and faithful practitioners. This level of teaching and practice, mastered and embodied by the great lineage masters such as Longchenpa, Jigme Lingpa, Patrul Rinpoche, and others, takes lojong to another level, one that can truly release the mind's habit at the level of grasping. In order to prepare ourselves to be practitioners capable of practicing at this level, we must become masters of lojong practice in this present moment. If we aspire to be true practitioners of the lineage teachings, we need to take the practice of lojong extremely seriously.

Avoiding Extremes

Something we are bound to face when we attempt to drop our emotions right on the spot is the temptation to fall into either the extremes of avoiding or digging in. What does this mean? We tend to do one of these two things when a strong emotion comes up. Most likely we do both, depending on the trigger and how we are feeling on a given day. Either we completely avoid the emotion, trying not to feel it at all, or we really dig into the emotion, trying to feel and get to know each and every part of it. Neither one of these extremes of behavior is what is meant by releasing an emotion when it arises.

We can see that within these two extremes is the tendency to either not look at the emotion at all or to stare at it long and hard. Let's take the example of training the mind in the illusory or dreamlike nature of the emotion to see how these two extremes manifest. First, if we try to avoid the emotion altogether, we immediately compartmentalize. Our reaction to the first movement and sensation of the emotion in the body is to shut it down, or shut it away somewhere where it won't be felt. We may think that this will result in a kind of mental and emotional stability. Indeed, this may be a behavior that we developed to allow us to keep our emotions from overwhelming us. However, it does not achieve the goal of lojong practice.

The goal of lojong practice is to be willing to see every expression of our own self-cherishing so that we can reverse our ordinary selfish tendencies and fearlessly develop the courage to put others before ourselves. But what happens when we avoid our emotions? We disconnect from what is happening. When we disconnect, how can we maintain our connections with others? And how can we really do away with self-cherishing? Actually, avoiding our emotions is just reinforcing another kind of attachment—the attachment to feeling comfortable and to not feeling emotional pain. This kind of numbness to feeling cannot give rise to genuine experiences such as compassion, loving-kindness, bodhichitta, and wisdom.

Wisdom and compassion are vivid, warm, energetic qualities of the mind. When we avoid looking at what is arising in the mind, we shut all our energy down. Having attachment to not feeling our emotions is just another kind of habit. It is just another face of emotional attachment. We should be clear that this is not the practice or the goal of meditation or the Buddhist path.

What about diving into the emotion? This is the habit we have been mainly trying to counteract through our practice of lojong.

When we dive into the emotion, we are already so overpowered by the experience of the emotion that we have no chance to release it. It has already caught us, and now we will have to work to get ourselves free. It is going to take a lot of our energy to pull ourselves back out, energy that we could have used for practice or to put forth some positive energy into our communities and environment.

Seeing the impermanent nature of the emotion as it arises takes a much lighter touch than either of these approaches. According to the lineage instructions given by the great Longchen Nyingthig master Minyak Kunzang Sonam, the previous incarnation of Tsara Dharmakirti Rinpoche, we must follow three steps in order to release our emotions more quickly: (1) recognize the emotion itself, (2) apply an antidote, and (3) commit to following through.

1. RECOGNITION

Recognition is the essence of lojong practice. The ability to recognize when an emotion has arisen within the mind relies upon mindfulness. The Vajrayana tradition describes mindfulness as having two aspects. First, there is the quality of remembering. We must be able to remember the instructions that we have been taught and when we are supposed to use them. The second is the quality of introspection, the mind's watchful quality. It is sometimes likened to a shepherd who is making sure that no harm comes to his or her flock. If we have proper mindfulness, we catch the arising of emotional patterns and then recall exactly what we should do to release them. Of course, the difficulty we face is that we are not good at catching our emotions early. Ordinarily, a great deal of time will have passed before we realize that we are engaging in emotional patterns. Nonetheless, if we train the mind earnestly in recognizing that emotions have arisen, we will become more and more skilled at it.

Training the mind in recognition is the key to understanding why releasing our emotions is not the same as avoiding them. To recognize emotions have arisen within the mind, we must look directly at them. If we avoid the emotions, bury them, or put them into a box where we can't see them, we have not looked at the emotions at all. We have simply protected ourselves from feeling their effects. If we withdraw, isolate, or avoid knowing what is happening inside of us, we should pray for the willingness to look at the feelings and patterns that are arising within us. If we cannot begin to break down this pattern of avoiding and compartmentalizing, our practice of lojong will become stuck and we will notice no great improvement in ourselves at all.

Our beginning efforts at recognition are going to be difficult and may sometimes seem disappointing. In a given day we may not notice any of our emotions arising until it is much too late to temper our habitual reactions. Or we may notice a strong emotion—for example, anger—arise within the mind and then notice how quickly and effortlessly we pursue it. We may wish to work with the anger and be unable to. Or we may see how we are completely unwilling to work with lojong practice at all in the face of how justified our anger seems. We are going to have many days and many experiences like this. After all, we have been developing and acting out our emotional patterns since we were children. A few days, months, or even years may not make a huge difference in how we feel, act, and react. But if we stay with it and keep trying to recognize our own patterns, sooner or later we will change.

The ability to recognize when an emotion arises is the key to gaining more confidence as practitioners. When we see ourselves really striving to change ourselves, we can begin to feel a sense of trust in ourselves and in our practice. None of us is perfect. In the beginning, we may make many attempts and only have a few successes. But we can measure our growth by our willingness to open up, to see what is happening in the mind and body for what it is, and persevere in lojong practice. Only when we truly begin to see our self-cherishing for what it is, and notice when it has arisen, will we even have a chance to change our most fundamental habits.

2. APPLICATION OF THE ANTIDOTE

The application of an antidote relies upon the remembering quality of mindfulness. Once we have recognized that an emotion has arisen in the mind, we must immediately be able to recall how we are supposed to apply our lojong practice. Otherwise, what relief can mere recognition of the emotion provide? For example, simply noticing "I'm angry" may give us a sense of self-awareness and our self-cherishing, but it doesn't give us any way to move through the pattern that has manifested.

Again, we can use the example of reflecting on the illusory nature of our emotions. At the same moment that we recognize "I'm angry," we also recall the example of the magician's trick. We might think, *This whole situation is just something conjured up by my mind. There is no reason to hold on to it. Nothing is the way I think it is. I'm seeing everything through the lens of my self-attachment and my emotional habits.*

Breathing is also an important part of applying any antidote. When emotional patterns come up, the breath tends to get stuck somewhere in the body. Our respiratory rate generally rises and our breathing becomes shallower. When we notice this, we should attempt to breathe more deeply, pulling the breath down into the abdomen if we can. Then, keeping watch on the breath, we can continue to apply whatever lojong technique we are working with.

As we apply the antidote, we will probably notice that a single application of the antidote is only helpful for a period of time. When patterns of thoughts and emotions arise, they do so in waves. When we feel anger, for example, we may have the energy to recognize it the first time, to work with the breath, and to see it as something conjured by our self-cherishing. But even though the energy of the anger wanes, it often returns. We will have to make diligent effort to recognize and apply an antidote each time the pattern expresses.

We may notice that while we have the intention of doing this, our implementation of recognition and applying antidotes lacks endurance. In the beginning, we are able to catch the pattern and try to release, or at least temper, its expression. But we will also likely notice that this can sometimes become harder as time goes on, and the pattern expresses successive times. Just like marathon runners, we must train in these skills of recognition and application. We must commit to training even when we are tired and aren't sure we can go much further. By doing so we will slowly gain the strength to apply our lojong practice for longer periods of time. Eventually we will have to have more endurance than the patterns and the emotions, in order to release them.

Remember that we must wear the armor of patience when we practice on the path of lojong. Armed with patience, there is no skill too difficult to master and no foe too strong to defeat.

3. COMMITMENT TO PERSEVERE

Making a commitment to not repeat our emotional patterns is an essential part of trying to change them. For example, when we notice that we have become angry, we should apply the antidote and then think, *This pattern hurts me and others too much. No matter what, I'm not going to let myself get angry again.*

Some of us may hesitate to make this kind of commitment in the face of deeply rooted patterns. We may think that it is self-defeating. After all, which one of us is able to make a promise to not become angry and keep it? When we make commitments that we can't keep, we are in danger of using the broken commitments as ammunition for self-hatred and excuses to give up. Another reason we may resist applying an antidote is that some of us may still be struggling with the feeling that our emotions are sometimes justified and necessary to keep ourselves safe. Because we are unwilling to let go of this attachment to anger, we are also unwilling to commit to not becoming angry.

Lojong practice is essentially pragmatic. Our goal in this practice is to stop ourselves from tipping over the domino that is going to set off a chain reaction that will send waves of emotional energy through the body, which will then give rise to destructive thoughts, words, behaviors, and moods. If we stay focused on that goal, we need not become seduced or derailed by these other thoughts and ideas.

In light of this, what kind of purpose does making a commitment to not become angry in the future serve? It is another type of mind training, not unlike the way we train the mind in bodhichitta. When we begin to train in bodhichitta, we are also training in something impossible. How are selfish beings like us truly going to put others first? If we are really honest, we don't always want to put others first or think they deserve to be put first. At the early stages of bodhichitta practice, even treating others as equal to ourselves is incredibly difficult. But as we recall our commitment to bodhichitta over and over again and work with the techniques of lojong practice, our self-cherishing begins to loosen little by little, and we see progress. So, based on our commitment, our bodhisattva vow, something that starts as impossible can become possible.

The commitment we make to not give rise to strong emotions is just like this. It is something truly impossible in the beginning. On some days we may not be truly willing to make this commitment. But as the days, months, and years pass, and we see how powerless we are in the face of our emotional patterns, our conviction can become stronger. Our wish to put these habits aside and fully release them begins to build. This provides further energy to deepen our skills in recognition and the application of an antidote.

Lineage masters, lojong masters, and great bodhisattvas all trained in just this way. Gradually, in stages, they trained in the aspiration to benefit others and made commitments to abandon harmful thoughts, emotions, and habitual tendencies. Over time their training led to the perfection of those commitments and the blossoming of compassion and wisdom.

Using the Past and Future to Avoid the Present

Another way that we often avoid applying lojong to the thoughts and emotions is by obsessing about situations in the past and what may occur in the future. We are often preoccupied by our fears, regrets, and resentments of the past, which can cause us to project into the future, wondering how we can stop similar things from happening again. We all have experiences that we hope to avoid repeating in the future. Maybe they have to do with relationships—maybe we are always attracted to the "wrong" kind of person. Maybe we are tempted by behaviors that we know are self-destructive, such as overeating. Maybe we have experienced trauma in the past and, as a result, fear and anxiety come up whenever we step out of our ordinary routines. No matter what has happened to us in the past, we should never forget that all our experiences are equal in the eyes of lojong. Lojong can purify and transform all of them. When we face strong patterns arising in the moment, we can sometimes forget that the most powerful tool we have is our lojong practice and this present moment.

Lojong practice is the supreme way to purify the patterns that invite cyclical suffering to repeat in our lives. When we start to get a sense of déjà vu, thinking, *Here we go again*, we might find ourselves immediately getting lost in plans to help ensure that the same old patterns won't repeat. Instead we could focus on the dreamlike nature of all phenomena and notice our own attachment to the patterns that are arising within and without us. After all, if our attachment to the patterns and the emotions can be released, the patterns have no way to repeat themselves. Hearing this said by someone else does not make it real to us. But we can make this amazing discovery for ourselves if we are willing to apply lojong with diligence.

It isn't just because of difficulties in the past that we focus on the future. It is also because we haven't yet accepted that life is full of difficulties and pain that cannot be avoided. We all have experienced pain in the past. Our present is also full of pain and dissatisfaction, which we are either feeling now or will feel imminently. We may see the dissatisfactory nature of life at this moment, and we may feel crushed by the weight of it. Or we may feel some sort of temporary elation or joy that we are desperate to keep. If we stubbornly persist in the belief that this happy situation will continue, we will face the suffering of change when it comes as well as the emotional suffering brought on by our unwillingness to accept the changing nature of life.

The future seems to be our only hope. On its flip side, the very act of hoping invites an incredible amount of fear. We have so many heavy expectations. *I have never found the key to happiness before, but if I plan well enough and do things just right in the future, won't happiness finally be in reach?* Even as we think this, we may be consciously or subconsciously filled with doubt. *But what if it isn't? What if things turn out even worse than they are now?* Focusing on the future will agitate the mind and set our thoughts and emotions running, such that we have no way to relate to what is going on right now. Although what we want most is to not let the pain of the past wrangle its way back into us, when we are distracted by our hopes and fears, our deepest and most elusive patterns are sure to show their faces. This is how the foe of our emotional patterns strikes us right in the heart.

When we look ourselves straight in the eye, we probably realize that there is no way we will be able to control each and every detail so that our dream of happiness unfolds. But these daydreams certainly numb some of the pain of this moment, which sometimes seems unbearable.

In *Words of My Perfect Teacher*, Patrul Rinpoche tells a story to point out the futility of focusing too much on the future. A poor man by chance found a large sack of barley. He tied it to a rafter on the roof above him and laid down beneath it to plan what wonderful things would unfold because of his newfound fortune. He dreamed that he would become rich and that he would finally be able to marry. Once he was married, he and his wife would have a son. While he was contemplating the name of his future son, the sack of barley fell from the rafter and struck him dead.

What a dramatic story! Does this story mean that we should give up all notion of planning for the future? Of course not. Our modern society demands that we take care of our own needs, and that we spend some of our time and energy planning for how we will take care of ourselves for the duration of our lives. But at the same time we should recognize that the happy future that we are planning to escape to may never come. If we spend too much time and energy planning for the future, we lose any chance we have to be the masters of the present. If we hope too much, and put too much of our energy into thinking about the things we want, we will never learn the skill of accepting what we have, and we will lose the opportunity to appreciate and enjoy it.

Taking Off Our Emotional Glasses

The tradition of the Secret Mantrayana places an emphasis on seeing purely. We might wonder what this means, in ultimate terms as well as for those of us who are training in the path of lojong. For realized masters of our tradition, such as the omniscient Longchenpa, seeing purely has a very literal meaning. Such realized masters have cut through all self-cherishing completely. There is no fixation on "I" or "mine," and there is no reference point of the self at all. Their experience of samadhi is continuous. As a result, they do not experience the suffering of ordinary beings. Rather, their experience of the ordinary world is sometimes described as being as delightful as a beautiful garden. Because they have trained long and hard in the mind of bodhichitta, they effortlessly and spontaneously know how to benefit others, and they do so continuously with relaxed and loving minds.

As we train on the path of lojong, we should beware of our expectations. We cannot expect anything like the realization of the lineage masters to dawn within us suddenly. Ordinary life is not going to immediately lose its dissatisfactory nature. But what we will experience is the gradual ability to see situations more clearly and purely.

When we are in the midst of strong emotional patterns, it is as though we are wearing colored glasses. Everything we think, feel, sense, and perceive is influenced by the color of our glasses. What does this mean to us? Our self-cherishing is like a colored overlay on the mind. It causes us to take everything personally. It causes us to insert ourselves everywhere. As we begin to purify our self-cherishing even the tiniest bit, we will notice that our colored glasses are also becoming a bit less tinted. Maybe we insert ourselves into situations less forcefully or for shorter periods of time before we notice that the things happening around us are not all about us.

Over time, more and more of the tint on our glasses fades away. We begin to relax. When we talk to people, we hear what they say more clearly. We don't only think about what they are saying, but we take in the context of the words and discern what might be behind them. We see more of what is going on with them and less of what is going on with us—or there simply *is* less going on with us. When we enter a room, we are aware of our own energy and the energy of others. We don't take the feeling in the room personally. We try to collect ourselves, and not to impose how we feel on others. We see the flow and movement of the environment around us. When someone criticizes us, we look for truth in their words instead of defending ourselves. We change what we can and let go of what we can't. When we feel the need to criticize others, we look inside at how we are feeling. We manage our own energy and evaluate whether we should or shouldn't say what is on our minds. When we are hurt because our loved ones didn't do something the way we wanted it done, we reflect on how even if they had done what we wanted, we would probably still be disappointed with some aspect of their effort—because *that's how we human beings are.*

For practitioners of lojong, this is a step toward pure vision. Rather than seeing ourselves everywhere, we begin to see others for who they are. We begin to see how much room we have been taking up and how we have failed to make room for others all along. Once we begin to see others for who they are rather than letting our view of them be colored by our self-cherishing, we will find that all our relationships begin to improve. We will naturally become more compassionate and patient because we have gained the ability to see the pain and hardship of others. We will also rejoice in their happiness when they share it with us. We will have more to share with others. Rather than being constantly preoccupied with ourselves and assessing whether or not whatever is happening is okay with us, we will drop our expectations and just work at connecting with others the best we can in the moment.

Sharing Our Love

Ultimately the practice of lojong is about sharing the love we have with others. It is about gradually unearthing our warm hearts and being willing to stop protecting ourselves enough to let others in. Once we begin to train in lojong practice, we will surely recognize it as our lifelong friend. Only this friend has the ability to be there for us no matter what because it is inseparable from our own minds and hearts. Only this friend can teach us how to undo all the painful habits that keep us stuck, isolated, and disconnected because it works on the deepest, most ingrained parts of ourselves, the parts we know better than anyone else. Only this friend can help us follow the unmistaken, authentic spiritual path, the same path that so many masters have successfully followed before us.

Will we experience failures on the path of lojong? Yes, probably too many to count. But success in lojong practice is a direct result of getting it wrong, which gradually and patiently transforms into getting it just right. As we train in this way, we will find that the path itself becomes the reward. We are not merely working toward some unattainable future. We have the possibility in each and every moment to free ourselves completely from the tangled web of emotion that has enslaved us for so long. Each time, each moment we experience a glimpse of that freedom, we have liberated ourselves from unnecessarily heaping further suffering onto ourselves and others. Surely, this is cause for celebration.

Appendix: The *Heart Sutra*

T HE FOLLOWING WORDS are not part of the *Heart Sutra* but are often recited beforehand.

> Homage to the mother of the Victors of the three times—
> To the perfection of wisdom beyond thought and
>   expression,
> Unborn, unceasing, in the nature of space,
> The object of the exalted wisdom which knows itself.

THE *HEART SUTRA*

In the Indian language: *Bhagavatīprajñāpāramitāhṛdaya*

In the Tibetan language: *bCom ldan 'das ma shes rab kyi pha rol tu phyin pa'i snying po*

[In the English language: *The Essence of the Perfection of Wisdom, the Victorious*]

One section
Homage to the Perfection of Wisdom, the Victorious.

Thus I have heard. At one time the Victor was at Vulture's Peak near Rajgir together with a great assembly of the fully ordained and a great assembly of Bodhisattvas. On that occasion the Victor was absorbed in a concentration on the diversity of phenomena called "profound appearance." Also at that time the Bodhisattva, that great being, the exalted and powerful Avalokiteshvara was contemplating the profound practice of the perfection of wisdom, and he saw that the five aggregates, too, are empty of any inherent nature. Then, through the power of the Buddha, the venerable Shariputra asked the Bodhisattva, that great being, the exalted and powerful Avalokiteshvara, "How should any child of the noble lineage who wants to perform the profound activity of perfecting wisdom proceed?"

. . .

The Bodhisattva, that great being, the exalted and powerful Avalokiteshvara answered the venerable Shariputra, saying, "Any sons or daughters of the noble lineage who want to perform the profound activity of perfecting wisdom should consider things in the following way. They should clearly see that the five aggregates also are empty of any inherent nature. Form is empty. Emptiness is form. Emptiness is not other than form and form is not other than emptiness. Similarly, feelings, discriminations, compositional factors, and consciousnesses are also empty. Likewise, Shariputra, all phenomena are empty. They have no defining characteristics; they are unproduced; they do not cease; they are unstained; they are not separate from stains. They do not decrease nor do they increase.

. . .

"This being so, Shariputra, in emptiness there are no forms, no feelings, no discriminations, no compositional factors, no consciousnesses; no eyes, no ears, no nose, no tongue, no body, no mind; no visual forms, no sounds, no smells, no tastes, no tactile sensations, no mental objects. From the eye element to the mental element, right through to the element of mental consciousness—all do not exist. There is no ignorance and no ending of ignorance right through to no aging and death and also no ending of aging and death. In the same way there is no suffering, no source of suffering, no cessation, no path, no wisdom, no attainment, and no lack of attainment.

. . .

"Therefore, Shariputra, since Bodhisattvas have no attainment, they depend upon and dwell in the perfection of wisdom. Since their minds are without obstructions, they have no fear. Going beyond all distortions, they finally reach the state beyond sorrow, the culmination.

. . .

"All Buddhas of the past, present, and future have depended, do, and will depend upon the perfection of wisdom, through which they become unsurpassable perfectly and completely awakened Buddhas.

. . .

"Therefore, the mantra of the perfection of wisdom is a mantra of great knowledge. It is an unsurpassable mantra, a mantra comparable to the incomparable. It is a mantra that totally pacifies all suffering. It will not deceive you, therefore know that it is true! I proclaim the mantra of the perfection of wisdom: *DAYATA (OM) GATE GATE PARAGATE PARASAMGATE BODHI SWAHA.* Shariputra, it is in this way that Bodhisattvas, those great beings, train themselves in the profound perfection of wisdom."

. . .

Then the Victor arose from his concentration and expressed his approval to the Bodhisattva, that great being, the exalted and powerful Avalokiteshvara, "Well said, well said! Son of the noble lineage, that is just how it is, just how it is. The profound perfection of wisdom should be practiced exactly as you have explained it. Then the Tathagatas will rejoice."

. . .

When the Victor had spoken these words, the venerable Shariputra and the Bodhisattva, that great being, the exalted and powerful Avalokiteshvara, and the entire gathering as well as the worlds of gods, humans, demi-gods, and celestial musicians rejoiced, and they praised what the Victor had said.

. . .

Colophon
This concludes the Mahayana sutra known as *The Essence of the Perfection of Wisdom, the Victorious*. It was translated by the Indian abbot Vimalamitra and by the fully ordained translator Rinchen Dey. It was revised and finalized by the fully ordained great reviser and translator Namka and others. The excellently revised [version] was written on the wall of Geygyey Chema Ling in the temple [complex] Lhungyi Drupa of glorious Samyey.

This is from *The Heart Sutra: An Oral Teaching* by Geshe Sonam Rinchen, translated and edited by Ruth Sonam (Boston: Snow Lion, 2003). Used by permission.

About the Authors

ANYEN RINPOCHE is a tulku from Tibet of the Nyingma (Longchen Nyingthig) tradition. He is the author of *The Union of Dzogchen and Bodhichitta, Dying with Confidence, Journey to Certainty, Momentary Buddhism*, and with Allison Choying Zangmo, *The Tibetan Yoga of Breath*. He founded the Orgyen Khamdroling Dharma Center and lives in Denver, Colorado.

ALLISON CHOYING ZANGMO is Anyen Rinpoche's spiritual partner, personal translator, and a longtime student of both Rinpoche and his root lama, Kyabje Tsara Dharmakirti. She lives in Denver, Colorado.